PRESENTED TO

_____

BY

_____

ON THIS DATE

_____

LOVE DOES

for kids

LOVE DOES

for kids

BOB GOFF

LINDSEY GOFF VIDUCICH

ILLUSTRATED BY MICHAEL LAURITANO

Tommy
NELSON®

An Imprint of Thomas Nelson

Published in Nashville, Tennessee, by Tommy Nelson. Tommy Nelson is an imprint of Thomas Nelson. Thomas Nelson is a registered trademark of HarperCollins Christian Publishing, Inc.

The author is represented by Alive Literary Agency, 7680 Goddard Street, Suite 200, Colorado Springs, Colorado 80920, www.aliveliterary.com.

Tommy Nelson titles may be purchased in bulk for educational, business, fund-raising, or sales promotional use. For information, please e-mail SpecialMarkets@ThomasNelson.com.

Any Internet addresses, phone numbers, or company or product information printed in this book are offered as a resource and are not intended in any way to be or to imply an endorsement by Thomas Nelson, nor does Thomas Nelson vouch for the existence, content, or services of these sites, phone numbers, companies, or products beyond the life of this book.

Illustrated by Michael Lauritano and Diane Le Feyer.
Cover design by Connie Gabbert.

ISBN-13: 978-0-7180-9522-2

Library of Congress Cataloging-in-Publication Data

Names: Goff, Bob, author.
Title: Love does for kids / Bob Goff, Lindsey Goff Viducich ; illustrated by Michael Lauritano.
Description: Nashville : Thomas Nelson, 2018. |
Identifiers: LCCN 2018032662 (print) | LCCN 2018033319 (ebook) | ISBN 9780718095239 (ebook) | ISBN 9780718095222 (hardcover)
Subjects: LCSH: Christian life--Juvenile literature.
Classification: LCC BV4501.3 (ebook) | LCC BV4501.3 .G6463 2018 (print) | DDC 248.8/2--dc23
LC record available at https://lccn.loc.gov/2018032662

Printed in the United States of America

18 19 20 21 22 LSC 10 9 8 7 6 5 4 3 2 1

Mfr: LSC / Crawfordsville, IN / November 2018 / PO #9494666

CONTENTS

PROLOGUE

When God planned His great caper to save the whole world, do you know who He picked to do it? A little kid. The child's name was Jesus, and He grew up in a town called Nazareth. I bet Jesus went to school, helped His parents with chores, and played outside, just like you. Do you know what was amazing about Jesus, though? He wasn't just an ordinary kid. He was "God with us," here on Earth.

Before Jesus was born, I imagine that God saw lots of sad things in the world. I bet He saw that the people He created and loved had forgotten who they really were, and He probably thought of lots of ways to make things right again. God could have picked someone well-known or popular or powerful to lead everyone back to Him, but He didn't. God chose to rescue the world through a little boy. The boy became a teacher when He grew up, and He traveled with His friends, healing people and telling them the exciting news that God had come to save them and be with them.

One day, Jesus' friends asked what the kingdom of heaven is like. "Jesus," one of them worked up the courage to ask, "in Your kingdom, who will be the greatest?"

At the time, Jesus' disciples didn't quite understand the difference between someone being powerful and someone being important, and that those aren't necessarily the same thing.

Jesus looked over and saw a little kid who was listening in on their conversation. He called the child over and placed His hand on the little one's head. I can picture Jesus smiling a little. His friends were always asking Him questions like this, but Jesus never seemed to mind.

"Friends," Jesus said, "I'm going to tell you the truth. Unless you change and become like little children, you will never enter the kingdom of heaven. In My kingdom, the most humble people—the ones who are like this child—will be the greatest!"

Those words are still true today. Jesus' friends worried about which of them would be first in line and who was God's favorite. But Jesus came to teach His friends a whole new way of thinking, a way that seemed backward and upside down. Jesus' kingdom is about the things that are really important—things like faith, grace, love, and forgiveness. In Jesus' kingdom, the people with the most power are actually the ones with the most humility, and the leaders are those who serve others. Jesus' kingdom is for people with hearts like children—people who trust God to provide for them like a good dad would. Jesus came to let us know that we can bring all our imagination and whimsy to Him and He will give us pure hearts in return.

This book is for kids, big and small. This book is about the new kingdom Jesus invites us all to be part of—a kingdom we can enter only if we are *just like kids*. In the kingdom of heaven, we are all becoming a little more like children and a little more like love—and learning a little more about what love does.

1

MISTAKES

When I was in kindergarten, we had nap time every afternoon. I know, it sounds so boring, right? I thought so too. The only thing I liked about nap time was a special job I hoped to get. Every day, the teacher would pick someone to be the "Wake-Up Fairy." The Wake-Up Fairy got to put on wings, tap people on their shoulders with a magic wand, and announce that it was time to wake up. I thought it was the coolest job in the world, and I couldn't wait for my turn.

One day, my moment finally came—my teacher picked *me* to be the Wake-Up Fairy! *It's finally my chance! I'll be the best Wake-Up Fairy the world has ever seen*, I thought to myself.

I put on the fairy wings, grabbed the wand, and headed around the room to do my job, but I was so excited that I forgot to walk carefully. As I ran through the classroom, tapping my friends on their shoulders, *I stepped on somebody's nose*. My teacher wasn't happy. In fact, I'd had so much trouble listening and following directions that she took away my wand and wings.

To tell you the truth, it felt pretty awful. I didn't mean to hurt anyone; I was just so excited to do my job that I forgot to look where I was going.

Has that ever happened to you? Have you ever tried your

hardest to do the right thing but messed up anyway? We've all messed up now and then, and it can feel pretty awful.

What I learned later in life from Jesus is that when we mess up, we don't have to keep feeling awful. When Jesus picked out His friends and asked them to spend time with Him, He didn't go to the people who were the smartest in school or the most popular. He didn't even look for the people with fancy jobs or nice houses or those who made a lot of money. He definitely didn't look for people who always listened to their teachers or the ones who hadn't made mistakes before.

The Bible says Jesus saw a few fishermen near the edge of a lake and chose them to be His closest friends. I bet those fishermen had so much trouble in school that they didn't even go anymore! They probably didn't even have their nets on the right side of the boat most of the time, but Jesus picked them anyway.

Jesus asked a tax collector to follow Him too. Nobody liked tax collectors because they stole other people's lunch money and called it their own. In fact, Jesus spent so much time with people who had made big mistakes that people started saying not-so-nice things about Jesus behind His back. But Jesus didn't care what it would look like if He loved people who had made mistakes. He wanted everybody who had ever messed up to know that He liked them all the same. He even used their mistakes to prove how much He really loved them.

It's sometimes easy to think that when we make a mistake we are somehow a little less worthy of being loved, or that when people think about us they'll only think about the mistake we made. What I didn't realize when I made my big mistake in kindergarten is that God's love for us doesn't change on our worst days. Come to think of it, we can't earn more of God's love on our best days. We are simply loved by God, no matter what, and because of Jesus, God doesn't define us by our mistakes.

That day as the Wake-Up Fairy wasn't my only bad day at school. School was always hard for me, and at times I wanted to quit. But you know what? I didn't. I believed that Jesus loved me even when I struggled because the stories I read about Jesus showed He didn't see people for their mistakes. He saw them for who they were becoming, even when they couldn't see it for themselves.

What I didn't know as a failed Wake-Up Fairy was that someday, if I kept at it, I would go to school to become a law-yer. I would get the chance to help kids around the world by starting new schools that they could go to. And the one rule we have for students at our schools is this: we always try our best, but when we make mistakes, we remember how much Jesus loves us—no matter what!

Jesus knew that mistakes don't keep people from doing important things. Remember those fishermen He met by the lake? They would end up traveling all over, telling people about Jesus. And the tax collector? He eventually started a church. Can you believe that? All of this happened because Jesus told each of His friends who they were becoming, and they believed Him. So the next time you make a mistake, just think to yourself: *I am loved, and I am God's . . . and I wonder who God is turning me into.*

Here's the answer:

You are becoming a helper.

You are becoming a leader.

You are becoming love.

2

ROOM RENT

I spent a lot of time at my Grandma Mary's house when I was growing up. I loved her because she really liked me and because she was always coming up with capers and mischief. Whenever I would visit, she'd have a project or two waiting for me. One day, we'd build a solar oven together by setting a cardboard box lined with tin foil out in the sun and make grilled cheese sandwiches. The next day, we'd make rock candy out of sugar and water and watch it grow on a string.

Grandma Mary never learned how to drive a car, so she rode a tricycle everywhere she went—even as a grown-up! Most weeks, I'd ride my bike to her house, and Grandma Mary would hop on her tricycle so we could ride to the hardware store together to buy supplies for the next project. I was a really active kid, and Grandma Mary delighted in running around after her red-headed, freckle-faced tornado of a grandson. (I think it was because she had more than a little tornado in her too.) One of my favorite activities was to gather every single pillow in her house and make a huge pillow pile in the living room. Grandma Mary and I would stand on the couch and jump into the pile together, rolling in the pillows and laughing so hard that tears ran down our cheeks.

Grandma Mary loved me so much that she even gave me

my very own room in her house. It wasn't fancy. It had only a bed and a desk with an antique sewing machine on it. In one of the desk drawers, Grandma Mary would leave me nickels and dimes. She called it "room rent."

"It's only right to pay you rent if I'm going to use your room for sewing while you're at school!" she said.

The funny thing is, I can't remember Grandma Mary ever sewing a thing! Even so, every time I went to her house, I'd race upstairs to check my room-rent drawer. I'd always find a handful of change, and then we'd set off on our bicycle and tricycle and head to the store to get a candy bar or the materials for our next project.

It's easy to think that loving people the way Jesus did means we have to do really big things for them—the kinds of things the whole world will see or people will write about in newspapers, talk about in the news, or make into a movie. Doing big things to love people is fantastic, but what I learned from Grandma Mary is that big love doesn't need to attract big attention. We need to give love away like we're made of it, and sometimes that comes out in the smallest, simplest acts of kindness.

It didn't make much sense for Grandma Mary to pay me rent for a room that was already hers. Why would you pay rent to a little kid when you own the whole house? Why would you give so much time to make one person feel so special?

Even though they may not have looked big to most people, Grandma Mary's simple acts of love shaped the person I grew up to be. I knew that I wanted to show the same kindness to my own kids one day and that I wanted to be the type of person who helps other people too. Because Grandma Mary gave me so much love, I learned how to give more love away!

Lots of things in Jesus' kingdom seem to be the opposite of what you'd expect. Jesus said that the people who weren't well-known would be leaders. He said that the people who were overlooked would actually be most noticed by Him. And in Jesus' kingdom, our small acts of love can help other people in really big ways. When we give our love away, we're not paying Jesus back for what He's done for us. It's actually just the opposite. It's like He's left room rent in our dresser drawer, and He can't wait to see how we'll use what He has given us to love others.

3

WORDS OF LIFE

When I was in elementary school, I played on a Little League baseball team. I wasn't very good at sports, but that didn't stop me from playing.

My teammates figured out early on that if I stood next to the plate and waited to get hit with the ball that was pitched, I would get an automatic walk to first base—and my team would probably get more points. One day, toward the end of the game, I had a choice to make: *Should I take a ball to the shoulder like I always do, or should I try to actually swing the bat and make a hit?* At the last moment, I closed my eyes, swung, and miraculously heard a dull *whap* as my bat connected with the ball. It was a home run! I raced around the plates, sliding victoriously into home plate. Our team won the game!

A week or so later, my mom came into my room and told me I had some mail. *Mail? For me?* I opened the big envelope and found a card inside. I think it was the first card I'd ever received in the mail, and it was shaped like an apple. *Are all cards shaped like apples?* I wondered. When I opened the card, I saw the words "You are the apple of my eye" printed inside. Underneath that was a handwritten note: "Wow, what a hit, Bob! You're a real ballplayer. Love, Coach."

I read the words again, over and over. *Me? A real ballplayer?* Part of me couldn't believe it, but the words sank in because of who they were from. I trusted my coach, and if he thought I was a real ballplayer, then maybe I was.

This was my first experience with just how powerful words can be.

After I grew up, I had a daughter named Lindsey, and she was scared of getting in trouble at school. If students forgot their homework or forgot to get a paper signed, the teacher would send home a note to their parents, and the thought of having a note sent home grew into a huge fear in Lindsey's mind. Sweet Maria and I had to sit down with Lindsey to talk about it. "Honey," we said in all seriousness, "we need you to *go get a note from your teacher.*"

What Lindsey didn't realize is that making mistakes is okay sometimes. The day Lindsey finally got a note, she climbed into the car after school in tears. "I got a note from my teacher," she cried. "I forgot to get my test signed!"

Do you know what Sweet Maria and I did? We cheered!

Instead of signing the note from the teacher like I was supposed to do, I wrote over the small, wrinkled paper in huge letters, "LINDSEY IS A GREAT KID!"

You see, this is what God's grace is like. Grace is Jesus writing "YOU ARE A GREAT KID" over the mistakes in your life. Because I'm Lindsey's dad, she trusted me when I said she was a great kid, the same way I trusted my coach when he said I was a real ballplayer. We can trust Jesus the same way.

Did you know that one of Jesus' disciples made a really big—HUGE—mistake one time? His name was Peter, and right before Jesus was crucified, Peter got scared and started telling people he didn't even know Jesus. He had promised to be friends with Jesus, but at Jesus' hardest moment, Peter wasn't that great of a friend at all.

Do you know what Jesus did later? He *forgave* Peter and told him, "Peter, you're a *rock*. When people look at you, they're going to think of Me. And I'm going to use you to start My whole church."

You're a real ballplayer. You're a great kid. You're a rock.

These are all such different words, and on their own they might not have much meaning. But when spoken with love at just the right moment, these words have the power to change everything—even to change your life. That's why it matters how we choose to use our words. We have the ability to be each other's mirrors, to reflect back to each other who we're becoming.

The words we say to one another have tremendous power, so let's make them words of life.

4

SHINY PENNIES

When I was little, I thought the candy store owner was the luckiest man in the whole world. He could have candy any time he wanted! I visited him regularly, bringing with me the coins I had collected from my room rent. Back then, most pieces of candy cost just a cent or two, so every time I had a few coins I would wander down to his store, walk around, and marvel at the jars of colorful candy lining the walls. I didn't want some of it; I wanted all of it!

After I had made my selection, I would place the candy on the counter by the cash register and put all the change I had next to it. Learning how to count money had been hard for me, but the shopkeeper was a kind, grandfatherly man who would lean over the counter and slowly help me count the coins, pausing to remind me what each one was worth. Most days, he would smile and nod after he got to the correct amount, scoop up the change that was his, and hand the rest back to me.

I usually didn't even make it out the door with my candy, and instead would sit in the shop while I ate it. I would watch the shopkeeper interact with other customers in the same gentle, kind way, pausing in his friendly conversations to count change, keep what was his, and return the rest.

One day, when I brought my candy and change to the counter, the candy store owner didn't smile after counting my change. Instead, he sighed and said, "I think we're one penny short."

I liked that he said *we* because it made me feel like I wasn't alone with my problem. After a moment, he said, "I have an idea."

The shopkeeper reached behind him and grabbed a bottle of vinegar, some salt, and a cleaning rag. He picked up one of my old pennies, poured a little vinegar on it, added a pinch of salt, and rubbed it with the cleaning rag. I leaned in as if I were watching a magic trick. Slowly, my penny turned from dull brown to a brilliant, shiny copper color.

The storekeeper looked up. "In my store," he said with a grin and a twinkle in his eye, "shiny pennies are worth double."

Now, I knew that shiny pennies weren't actually worth double, but I believed the shopkeeper that day because of who he was. Words spoken from kind people have the power to change everything. He liked me, and he owned the store, and he made up that rule just for me.

In many ways, we're like my old penny that I offered to the storekeeper. We aren't enough on our own, but God still decides to see us as incredibly valuable to Him. This is called *grace.* God's grace is a lot like the candy store owner with a cleaning rag, making us brand new.

The beautiful thing about grace is that we get to show it to others too. We can decide that people are worth a whole lot to us because they are also worth so much to God. We get to forgive people even when they hurt our feelings or take something away from us, and in this way we can show them what God is like.

We get to decide that shiny pennies are worth double.

5

I'M WITH YOU

People can get lost in lots of different ways. Sometimes they get confused about *where* they are, like getting lost in the grocery store. Other times they can feel lost because they're unsure about *who* they are. Some people even get amnesia and forget everything about themselves. They don't even remember their names! Can you imagine what that would be like? I've never forgotten my name before, but a couple times I've forgotten who God made me to be.

I already told you that I was never very good at school. Eventually, in high school, I decided that the best thing for me to do was to give up on school altogether. I decided I'd do what I had always wanted: move to the mountains in Yosemite (a big, beautiful national park) and become a forest ranger! I would climb mountains, live in a tent, and eat hot dogs and Pop-Tarts. I was sure it would be awesome. Looking back now, I can see that I was a little lost. I knew exactly where I was, but I didn't know who I was.

Before I left for the mountains, I went to see my friend Randy. Randy was a Young Life leader at my high school. He was a grown-up who liked to hang out with high school kids and tell them about Jesus. I wasn't sure about Jesus yet, but I really liked Randy, so I drove to his house to say good-bye.

As I told Randy my plan to move to the mountains, he didn't tell me what a bad idea it was or make me feel worse than I already did. (Deep down, I knew I should finish school.) Instead, he excused himself to get something from his room. After a few minutes, Randy came back to the front door. Do you know what he had with him? He had a backpack over one shoulder and a sleeping bag under his arm.

Randy didn't make a speech. Instead, he said what people who are lost need to hear from someone they trust: "I'm with you." He walked out to the car with me, put his sleeping bag on top of mine, and climbed into the passenger seat. Randy wasn't just saying that he was with me to be nice. He was actually *with* me in the car as we drove all the way to Yosemite. He told me that he would stay with me while I got settled into my new life and tried to find a job.

I didn't have much of a plan, but the little one I had started falling apart as soon as I arrived at Yosemite. I couldn't find a job or even a place to stay. Randy and I were too big to sleep in the car and too cold to sleep outside, so we snuck into an unused tent at a campground and slept there.

After just a few days at Yosemite, I told Randy with a sigh, "This isn't working out very well at all. Maybe I should just go back home and finish high school."

Once again, Randy said the same thing he'd been saying the whole time: "Bob, I'm still with you."

God made everyone who has ever been alive. That's a lot of people. He made us so we'd love Him. Sometimes it's hard to remember that. In fact, it wasn't long after He made us that we wandered away from Him. We were all lost, kind of like I was in high school. We'd forgotten who He made us to be—His people. So God made a plan to make things right in the world. He decided to send His Son, Jesus, to Earth, to be with us.

God doesn't try to talk us out of going on adventures, but He stays close to people who have forgotten who they are. He's with them the same way Randy was with me. And we get to do the same thing for our friends too. The next time your friends seem a little lost or like they've forgotten who they are, do what Randy did. You don't need to say a lot. Just tell them that you're *with* them—just like God is always with us—no matter what.

6

SAILING WITH YOUNG LIFE

When I was in college, I spent my summers volunteering for an organization called Young Life. People who volunteer for Young Life spend their time hanging out with high school kids on campus. They go to football games and other events after school and, over time, tell them about who Jesus is and who God made them to be.

One of my favorite things about Young Life is their summer camps. There are lots of Young Life camps that high school kids can go to. One summer, my friend Doug and I took a group of Young Life kids on a sailing trip in Canada.

About a dozen kids signed up for the boat trip, and they could not have been more different from each other. The group included football players and cheerleaders, artsy kids and rough kids, straight-A students and kids who were barely going to graduate. I'm not going to lie—the first day on the boat was more than a little awkward as the groups of kids scrambled to find the farthest distance from each other on the boat.

We set sail early in the morning, passed under the Lions Gate Bridge in Vancouver, and headed north. The strange thing about being at sea is that although you're in a relatively

small space that is dry and safe, you're completely surrounded by water a thousand feet deep. All around are waves and strong winds—and there's nowhere for you to go. Being on a small boat for a week can bring people together who otherwise might not seem to have much in common.

By the third day, we had sailed most of the way up a beautiful inlet ringed by mountains and glaciers. The sun broke through the clouds, and we anchored with the breeze in our faces. At the front of the boat was a huge, colorful sail called a "spinnaker." It was bigger than the whole boat! While we were at anchor, Doug and I figured out that if we hooked up a couple harnesses to the bottom of the spinnaker for the kids to sit in, they'd have quite a ride.

The kids took turns sitting in the harness while the sail filled with air, lifting them above the sea. They would soar up into the air, higher with each gust of wind, until the sail collapsed at about twenty feet, and the kids would come crashing down into the water. The students laughed so hard they cried, and their fun went on for hours. Suddenly, the fact that one kid was a star football player and another was unathletic and artsy didn't seem very important to anyone. I think God made it so that shared experiences—doing things together—brings people close, no matter how different they are.

It's no wonder that Jesus decided to spend so much time on boats with His disciples. You see, the disciples weren't football players or artists or cheerleaders, but they were equally different. Some were fishermen, and some were tax collectors. Some had gone to school for many years, and others probably hadn't gone at all. Some counted money for their jobs, while others spent their days wrestling smelly fish out of tangled nets. It's easy to forget how different they all were.

One time, Jesus took His disciples on a boat, and a huge storm raged all around them. The disciples were terrified and ran back to where Jesus was. They found Him on a cushion—*asleep.*

The disciples woke Jesus up in a panic. "We're going to die!" they yelled. "How can you be asleep?!"

Jesus stood up and, with the calm authority that comes only from being God, said, "Wind and waves, stop! Be peaceful." Immediately the storm stopped, and the Bible says the disciples stood in awe of Jesus.

I'd bet the disciples weren't the same after that boat trip.

I bet they elbowed each other and said, "Did you *see* that?!" I wonder if that moment of being in awe of Jesus together made them less aware of each other's mistakes or successes or differences.

When you're on an adventure with people, everything changes. Being surrounded by wind and waves, traveling through the beautiful world that God created, and hanging from the bottom of a huge spinnaker are the things that make our differences seem less important. When you stare at a huge mountain with sheer cliffs and waterfalls cascading thousands of feet, you forget that the person next to you smells a little funny or was mean to you once in second grade. God designed us to be this way. I think He knew that the more we stand in awe of Him, the less we'll stand in judgment of each other.

7

WEDDING CAKE

When Sweet Maria and I got married, we didn't have any money. Lots of people have flowers and steak at their weddings. When we asked around and found out they were too expensive, we weren't disappointed at all! We blew up a thousand rainbow-colored balloons and served up macaroni. The part of the wedding I cared about most (besides marrying Sweet Maria, of course) was the cake. At the time, we were both a part of Young Life, so we had a lot of high school friends. One of them said that his dad owned a bakery and they could make us a huge cake for next to nothing. I was sold.

When we got to the wedding reception, I saw that our friend was assembling the cake in the parking lot. It seemed like kind of a strange place to be stacking a cake, but the cake itself was magnificent—four layers, each held up with pillars. It was the most magical cake I'd ever seen—the kind of cake you dream about. I couldn't wait for all our guests to dig into it. Our young friend finished assembling the cake on a rolling cart and started pushing the cart across the uneven parking lot asphalt.

"Oh no . . ." my friend said. Just as we walked into the reception area, a wheel on the cart caught on a small rock.

In one horrible moment, the entire wedding cake fell on the ground.

Splat.

Splat.

SPLAT.

We were all part stunned, part amazed as we surveyed the damage. It was like we'd just had an epic cake and frosting food fight—and we didn't even get to throw any! The mess was remarkable. We had only a few moments before the guests arrived and no backup plan. We really needed to serve that cake! I sent Sweet Maria into the reception area and started scooping. My high school buddy and I smashed that cake back together the best we could, and then he raced to the bakery for more frosting.

A couple of buckets of frosting later, we had saved our cake (kind of), and—don't let any of our guests know this—we served it right up, *pebbles and all.*

Like that cake, our lives are full of small rocks and pieces of asphalt. We all have those times when we're clumsy, make mistakes, hurt someone's feelings, forget to do the right thing, or lose our tempers. None of these disqualify us from being used by God to love others. Jesus somehow makes us able to serve anyway. He doesn't ignore the areas of our lives where we aren't perfect, and He wants to help us with the things we're doing wrong. What He does is use us despite those imperfections.

All over the Bible are stories of Jesus spending time with people who had made really, really big mistakes. But do you know what Jesus compared His kingdom to? He said it was like a wedding party! He said the guests would be the imperfect ones because they realize just how much they need Jesus. And if we fall apart in the parking lot, Jesus will put us back together. He doesn't shake His head and start over again with someone else. He picks us back up and uses us, just the way we are.

8

PICTURES IN A WALLET

Here's something about me that you might not know: like most grown-ups, I carry around a wallet, but unlike most grown-ups, I carry around a really, *really* big wallet. It's huge! I keep it in my back pocket, and sometimes when I sit down in the car, I think I'll hit my head on the roof.

I use my wallet to hold all the normal stuff—my driver's license, a coupon to get some frozen yogurt, a couple of dollar bills—but do you know what makes my wallet so big? Pictures! My wallet is bursting at the seams with photographs of the people I love most. I fill my wallet with pictures of the important stuff in my life. There's no picture of my house or my car or my piggy bank. Those things aren't bad, of course. They're just not as good as pictures of family and friends.

The photos in my wallet are a little bent and tattered, but I like knowing that they're there. As I flip through my wallet to look for some money to buy a candy bar, I often catch a glimpse of the faces I love peeking out from behind a dollar bill, and it always makes me smile. It's as if they're saying, "Get one for me too!"

If you ask my kids, they'll tell you that all I ever want for Christmas is pictures of them. In fact, we joke that Christmas for me is always "flat Christmas" because all the presents under the tree with my name on them are flat. They're usually rectangles and have framed photos hiding beneath the shiny Christmas wrapping paper. You see, my family is what my whole life is about, and nothing is more special to me than having pictures of my wife, my kids, and even my dog to remind me of what's most important.

One Christmas, my children picked up a flat present from under the Christmas tree and walked it over to me together with huge grins. "You're going to love this," they said as they excitedly handed me the package wrapped in festive paper. It was thicker than the photos I usually get, and I could feel tears welling up in my eyes already because I knew it would be another picture of some of the people I love the most.

"It's a photo book!" The kids cheered as I peeled back the paper wrapping. It held pictures of all the adventures we had gone on together. It was a pretty thick book! Page by page, I flipped through the book and thought about our adventures and the things we had learned together along the way.

Happy tears streamed down my cheeks as I turned the last few pages of the book. When I got to the end, I was surprised to find an envelope attached inside the back cover. Inside the envelope I found three letters—one from each of my kids. But the letters weren't written to me. They were written to their future kids. The letters told stories about hope and love and adventures they hoped they'd go on together when they had children of their own.

Adam's letter read like this:

Dear future kids,

You'll see a lot of pictures in this book of the adventures we have gone on as a family. I can't wait to take you on adventures too. I hope you love Jesus and adventure as much as we did.

Love,

Your dad, Adam

I'm not sure if God carries a wallet, but if He does, I bet it's bursting at the seams with pictures of His kids—including you and me. Maybe as He made the whole world and put the stars in the sky to shimmer over us, He spread His pictures of us all over heaven's living room floor and thought to Himself, *They're going to love this place.*

Just like my kids wrote letters to their future kids, God also wrote us letters filled with stories of hope and love and invitations to adventures He hoped we'd go on with Him. These letters and stories were all put in one book we call the Bible. I don't know what God calls it, but my guess is that He calls it a book of what He hopes we'll do together with Him forever.

Sometimes it's easy to forget that when God thinks about you, He gets a big smile on His face. He didn't just create us; He really, *really* likes us too. Just like a proud dad who wants to show everyone pictures of his kids, maybe God is constantly calling the angels over to see pictures of us from His wallet. He tells them what we've been doing while we've been on Earth and what He hopes we'll do. He's been showing pictures of you around heaven so much that I bet the corners of some of the photos are a little bent and worn. But He doesn't care, because every day and with everything you do, He gets a new picture of you for His wallet.

9

UNICYCLE

Mom. Dad. I have a question," my son Richard announced with all the seriousness his seven-year-old voice could muster. "Could I have my birthday present early this year?"

Sweet Maria and I looked at each other in surprise and then turned back to Richard. It was January. His birthday was in June. Richard is the kind of kid who would pick the smallest cookie on the tray so you could have the biggest one, then convince you he wanted the small one anyway. Asking for an early birthday present was totally out of character for him. This had to be good.

"Tell us what you're thinking, buddy," I replied.

Richard launched into his story. Apparently, his second-grade class was putting on a carnival for the kindergartners at school, and every kid in the class had to choose something to perform in the carnival. When the teacher asked Richard what he wanted to do, he took a deep breath and proclaimed, "I want to ride a unicycle!"

Do you know what a unicycle is? It's kind of like a bicycle, but instead of having two wheels, it only has one. Unicycles are *really* tippy, and Richard had never ridden one in his life. He'd only even seen a unicycle once or twice before. It didn't occur to Richard to choose something he was great at to perform

in the carnival. Instead, he just thought of the coolest thing he could imagine and went for it. I love that about my son.

Richard's big idea created a big problem, of course, which is why he asked for an early birthday gift. Richard had exactly ten days to learn how to ride a unicycle for the school carnival, and he didn't even have one.

Richard broke his piggy bank open, and Sweet Maria and I agreed to help him with the rest of what he needed for an early birthday present. By that afternoon, Richard was practicing in our garage, teetering back and forth on a kid-size unicycle, gripping for dear life onto a rope we'd hung up. For the next ten days, you could find him in the garage, slowly pedaling across the concrete and improving his balance just a little at a time.

By the time the carnival rolled around, Richard could manage just a few shaky pedals forward before he fell. The kindergarten kids went wild, though, clapping and cheering. It didn't matter that Richard hadn't really mastered riding a unicycle—those shaky pedals forward were Richard's way of showing the kindergarten kids that they were loved and worthy of a performance, and that's all that mattered.

A lot of times, when we think about loving others and building Jesus' kingdom here on Earth, it's easy to believe that we need to have everything figured out before we get started. But we don't. When Richard's teacher asked him what he wanted to do for the carnival, Richard didn't stop to think about what he *couldn't* do or what he *didn't* have. Instead, he imagined the carnival trick that would make the biggest impact, and he asked his parents for help and guidance in making it happen.

Did you know that we get to do the same thing? When you're thinking about how to show people love, go big. Imagine the most extraordinary thing you could do to love others, go to your heavenly Dad for help and advice, and pursue the creative dreams He has given you with everything you've got. In the end, God doesn't delight in our successes; He delights in our attempts. Anything we do to love others, even imperfectly, is one shaky pedal forward toward bringing God's kingdom here on Earth.

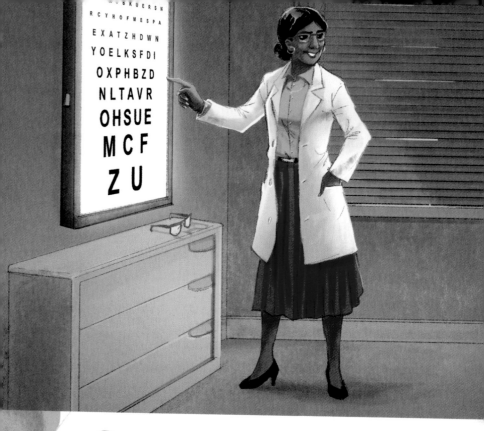

10

SEE A LITTLE MORE

From the moment I opened my eyes that morning, something felt a little funny.

Blink.

Blink. Blink.

I felt like I was wearing a pirate patch over one eye, which would have been really cool. But nothing was covering my eye. As if someone had flipped a switch, I suddenly couldn't see out of my right eye. I put my hand over my left eye, and everything was dark.

Now, it turns out that even though I wasn't great at school when I was a kid, I love to start schools. Over the past few years, I've gotten to travel around the world and work with some incredible people to open schools for kids. On this particular morning, I was in Iraq, meeting with some new friends and making plans for another school. This was a big trip, and I'd be visiting a couple other countries before heading home, so I figured I could get by with one eye and wait to see a doctor.

When I got back to San Diego, I finally went to visit my eye doctor. She's one of the best eye doctors in the whole world. When she heard that I'd kept traveling without getting my eye checked, she shook her head.

"Bob," she said. "You should have come to me sooner!"

Thankfully, my doctor was able to do surgery right away. The best part was that I got to wear a *real* eye patch afterward! I had to keep my eye covered with the eye patch for a few weeks, so I spent that time imagining how great it would be to see again.

The moment finally arrived for my doctor to take off the eye patch, but something surprising happened. I opened my right eye, but I still couldn't see very well! I didn't see complete darkness anymore, but the whole world still looked fuzzy, like when you open your eyes underwater.

"Wait!" I exclaimed in disbelief. "Why didn't the surgery work? I thought I'd be able to see again!"

"Bob," my doctor replied patiently. "Every day, you'll be able to see a little more."

"When will I *really* be able to see again?" I asked. Not knowing when my eye would be completely better made me a little uneasy. A lot of things I love to do, like driving cars

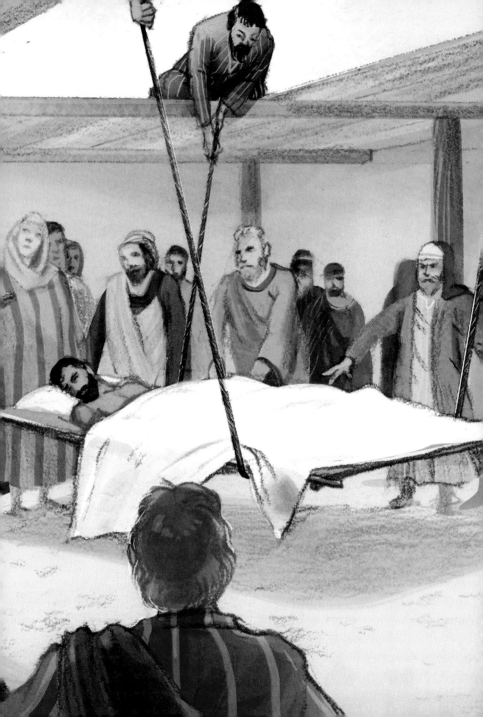

and flying airplanes, require both of my eyes. I didn't want to wait to do those things. I wanted to be better right away!

Over the next few months, I continued to visit my eye doctor for regular checkups. Each time, I asked her when I'd be able to see again, and her response was always the same: "Every day, you'll be able to see a little more."

The Bible tells lots of stories about Jesus spending time with people who were sick or couldn't see. One time, Jesus was walking with His friends when He met a blind man. Some of the blind man's friends had brought him to Jesus and begged Jesus to heal him. Jesus spit on the man's eyes and put His hands on him and then asked if he could see.

"I see people," the man said. "They look like trees walking around." When Jesus touched him again, the man could see clearly. I can relate a lot to that story now because I wasn't healed all at once either. I'm *still* seeing a little more every day.

Another time, there was a man who was so sick he couldn't even get out of bed. So, the sick man's friends picked up his bed and carried him all the way to the house where Jesus was teaching. When they got there, the friends discovered that the house was packed so full of people that they couldn't get through the door. Do you think that stopped them? No!

The man's friends decided to make a hole in the roof and lower their friend down. When they finished transforming the house into a convertible and got their friend in front of

Jesus, do you know what Jesus told the man? He didn't say, "You're healed!" and heal the man all at once. Instead He said, "Friend, you're forgiven." I don't think Jesus was just forgiving the man for the hole his friends made in the roof. You see, Jesus knew that healing the man's heart, way down deep, needed to happen before the rest of his body could be healed.

It has been really difficult for me to be patient as I wait for my eye to get back to normal. But you know what? I've noticed that Jesus is healing me on the inside while He's healing me on the outside. Even though my eye isn't seeing well yet, I'm learning to see a little better in other ways. I'm noticing where I need to be more patient and loving or where I need to help others. What I'm learning from Jesus and from my eyes is that Jesus really cares about all of us and wants to heal us inside and out. So, the next time you feel sick or hurt, ask Jesus to heal you on the inside *and* the outside—because He cares about all of you!

11

ZOO

When our kids were little, our house had more animals than the zoo. We didn't have a panda or a polar bear or an alligator, but not because we didn't try. We did have a tiny lop-eared rabbit named Ben who was black and white and looked like a soccer ball with floppy ears. We also had four Rhode Island Red chickens named Teriyaki, Colonel Sanders, Nugget, and Barbeque. (We called them Terri, Colonel, Nugget, and Barbie for short.) Even though we gave the chickens food names, we never ate them, of course. These chickens laid their eggs all over the yard, making every day like an Easter egg hunt.

Some of our favorite animals were our ducks. We didn't get them; they kind of got us. One day Sweet Maria was at the post office, and the man behind the counter seemed to be very upset.

"What's wrong?" Sweet Maria asked, concerned.

"Someone ordered baby ducks through the mail," the man responded, "but they haven't come to pick them up! They're barely two days old. Your family takes care of animals, right? Would you be able to give them a home?"

Sweet Maria thought about it for a moment and replied, "We'd love to."

When she opened the front door, the frantic *peep-peep-peep-peep-peep* of a dozen tiny, yellow, fluffy baby ducks filled the house. The kids quickly made a little home for our new friends in a large plastic bin, complete with a warm overhead light and fresh water. Our family got a little bigger that day, and you know what? We liked it better that way.

It wasn't long before the ducks grew up, sprouted white feathers, and spent their days in the backyard with the chickens and rabbit. The kids would carry the animals around the yard, feed them, and love them. And the animals loved the kids right

back. We knew everything about our animals' habits too. We knew what they liked the most, like eating snails, and what they feared the most, like our neighbor's dog. We knew what they were good at, like making messes, and what they were bad at, like math. We knew where they liked to play and all of their best hiding places in the bushes.

Every night, just as the sun went down, we would call the ducks and the chickens and the rabbit. They knew our voices and knew we would protect them, so they would all waddle, strut, or hop to the back door. We would count heads to make

sure everyone was there, and then we guided them into the shelters we'd made for them to stay in at night.

We never put a fence around our pets because they didn't try to run away. The chickens probably couldn't have flown away even if they wanted to, but the ducks could have. Do you know what, though? They never wanted to. The ducks happily waddled around the yard all day, staying close to each other and close to us, quacking up a racket. They knew the safest place for them to be was near us because we took care of them. If one did wander away from the yard by mistake, the kids would find it right away. If I had to guess, I bet the ducks never tried to wander away because they knew how bad it felt to be lost at the post office and how great it felt to be found by a loving family.

We've all got a little bit of adopted duck in us, in the sense that we know what it feels like to be lost. We may not have ended up in a box at the post office, but we all feel a little lost sometimes at home or at school or in our neighborhoods. We also know what it's like to be found. Think of a time you got lost in a crowd or at the store. Do you remember the panic you felt as you looked around for someone familiar? When your parents or friends found you, you probably let out a big sigh of relief. It's a great feeling—like being gently placed in a cozy bin with a warm light.

The Bible says that people around Jesus saw how good

He was at caring for others, and they brought many people to Him to be cared for. When Jesus explained God's love to His friends, He often gave examples about caring for animals like birds and sheep. Jesus said He knew what even the tiniest bird needed, and He said that if a sheep were lost, He would search until He found it. These stories made sense to my family because we knew what our ducks and chickens and rabbit needed, and we would go find them if they got lost too.

God knows everything about His kids—what we need and what we like and where we try to hide sometimes. He cares about us so much that He always comes to look for us when we're lost. Jesus told these animal stories because He wanted us to know the reason God sent Him to Earth. Just like the sheep, we were lost, and Jesus came to find us. Whenever I think about our pets and the way they stayed in our yard, I remember that the safest place for us to be is close to Jesus, listening for His voice and running to Him when He calls.

12

GIFTS

When I was a kid, I used to count down the days to my birthday. I'm sure you do too. I would dream of cake and ice cream and presents. Come to think of it, I still think about the cake and ice cream quite a bit, even when it's not my birthday. But as I got older and had my own kids, I started to think about birthday presents a little differently.

I stopped thinking about getting presents for myself because to be completely honest, my family was the only present I really wanted. So, one year I decided to do something different. The day before my birthday, Sweet Maria and I loaded the kids into the car, and I said, "Okay, guys, we have an important errand to run. We need to get some birthday presents for me!"

The kids were very confused. "Wait," Richard said, "why is Dad coming to get his own birthday presents?!"

Lindsey and Adam gave each other puzzled looks. Weren't birthday presents supposed to be surprises?

The kids grew even more confused as our car passed all the normal stores for buying grown-up birthday presents and we turned into the parking lot of their favorite toy store.

"Boys," I said, turning to Richard and Adam, "what I really want for my birthday are some NERF guns or a remote-control car like the one you've been hoping for! And Lindsey,

you've got to pick out a doll for me and also some shoes with sparkles on them—in your size!"

This became my new birthday tradition. We'd run up and down the aisles together, picking out baseballs and gloves and Lego sets and dolls and pogo sticks for the kids as *my* birthday presents. As the kids got older, the presents changed to things like clothes and music and snowboards. As a dad, all I wanted for my birthday was to watch my kids enjoy the things they loved and to share those moments with them. The reason was simple: the things that brought them joy brought *me* joy.

Do you know that the Bible talks a lot about gifts? For Jesus' first birthday, wise men brought gold and frankincense and myrrh as gifts. (I always wondered if Jesus secretly hoped He'd get a bicycle instead. I would.) God gives us special gifts, like friends, family, and experiences to enjoy. He likes to give away these kinds of gifts because the things that bring us lasting joy bring *Him* lasting joy too.

The Bible also talks about another kind of gift you don't get for your birthday or in a store. They're the kind of gifts that God places *inside* us. Some of the gifts are feelings, like hope and joy and happiness. Other gifts are the ability to do things, like serving people or being generous or helping people to understand who Jesus is.

The Bible talks about a man named Paul. He helped people figure out what it meant to follow Jesus after Jesus had gone back to heaven. Paul wrote about how God gives each person a special gift—something they are especially good at doing. He said the more we understand about our gifts, the more we'll know about God. Do you know why God gave us these gifts? Paul said they will help us love each other better and point each other toward Jesus.

As a dad, watching my kids find gifts they liked and then seeing them share the gifts with me and each other was the best present I could imagine. I think that God, who's our Father, might feel the same way about us. The gift we give to Him is enjoying the gifts He gives us and sharing them with others. We show Him how much we love Him by how much we love each other.

My friend Don said that God is a Dad who is leaning over our lives, excited to see what wonderful things we might create with what He has given us. I think Don's right. I think we also lean over each other's lives too. I never needed to tell my kids what I wanted them to get me because they already knew. I wanted their love. I wanted them to love the people around them. And if they wanted to get a toy car and some sparkly shoes too, all the better.

13

THE LETTERS

Our family's experience making friends all across the world began with some postage stamps—236 stamps, to be exact.

On September 11, 2001, something scary happened in the world. Some people decided to hurt others by making airplanes crash into buildings. I heard the news on the radio on my way to work in the morning, and I immediately turned the car around so I could go tell my kids. You see, our family didn't have a television, and if anything bad happened in the world, I wanted my kids to hear about it directly from their mom and dad.

Later that night, as we were talking at the dinner table about what had happened, I asked the kids, "If you could speak with a president or a prime minister right now, what would you say?"

The kids thought about it for a minute, and then Lindsey said, "Well, I would want to ask what gives the leader hope, and I would ask what they would say to encourage kids around the world."

Richard was starting to get interested in making videos, and he said, "I think it would be really cool to make a video of an interview that we could share with other kids."

Then Adam, the youngest, said, "I'd want to invite the presidents and prime ministers to come visit our house, and if they couldn't make it, maybe we could ask if we could go visit them at their houses!"

By the end of dinner, we'd hatched a plan. The kids decided they would write letters to every single world leader and ask if they could meet with them for a video interview about hope—and then share that message of hope with kids around the world. We'd also invite the leaders over to our house.

Lindsey, Richard, and Adam wrote their letters together. Hundreds and hundreds of them. We looked up the names and addresses of every world leader. The kids ended up writing to every king, queen, prince, princess, president, and prime minister on the planet.

We were wondering if any of the leaders would write back, and do you know what happened? Most of them did! The first letters that came in were very kind, and many included photos and bookmarks. But everyone said no to the kids' interview idea.

Then, one day, it happened. They got a yes! Eventually, more than twenty-five leaders agreed to meet with the kids. They invited Lindsey, Richard, and Adam to come to their houses, and even said that Sweet Maria and I could come along too. After sending a few more letters back and forth, we scheduled our meetings and got some plane tickets, and the kids were off on their adventure.

As we met with the leaders and made new friends, we noticed that many of them said the same thing: if a grown-up had asked them to meet, the leaders probably would have said no. They said that grown-ups usually show up to meetings with an idea about something they want the leaders to do or not do, instead of just wanting to be friends. When kids ask to be friends, though, that's really all it is: an invitation for friendship, with nothing expected in return.

Just like the leaders who said they'd meet with our kids, Jesus told His friends that He wanted to spend time with kids too. Kids just like you! One time, when Jesus was surrounded by grown-ups, some kids tried to get close to Jesus and talk to Him. The other grown-ups tried to shoo the kids away, saying that Jesus was too busy for them. But do you know what Jesus said? "Let the kids come to me!"

Jesus told the grown-ups that the new kingdom He was building on Earth isn't just for adults. Everyone is welcome, of course, but He said kids would be a *huge* part of what He was doing. In fact, He said that kids seemed to understand a lot of the things He taught better than some of the grown-ups did!

What I learned from my kids and from Jesus is that being friends with someone without expecting anything in return has the power to change the world. Grown-ups sometimes tell kids about all the things they can't do until they're older, but we need to remember that Jesus doesn't just like kids a lot—He wants to use them to teach adults how to have a childlike faith.

Whatever your age, you can help people understand how God want us to see the world. He wants us to see it the way a child would.

14

NO-MANNERS NIGHT

Do you have people in your life who try to teach you good table manners? Maybe your parents remind you to chew with your mouth closed during dinner or keep your elbows off the table or say *please* and *thank you*. These are great things to learn. Who knows? You might be the president someday, and you wouldn't want to put your feet on the table by mistake.

Knowing good manners is important, but sometimes it gets a little boring to practice good manners *all the time*. So I made a deal with my kids: if they could remember their good table manners for a whole week, we would have No-Manners Night.

We looked at our calendar and circled the week we would practice our best manners. Then we watched and waited as the date got closer. The week finally arrived, and do you know what happened? Our kids had terrific manners! They set the table with the knives and forks and spoons on the correct sides of the plates, and the boys pulled out the girls' chairs. No one even burped! They did great. No-Manners Night was on!

Sweet Maria and I made sloppy joes and spaghetti and Jell-O, and we ate all of it with *no manners*. Food flew everywhere. Sloppy joes were plopped on heads. Spaghetti was stuck

to the ceiling. Jell-O covered the chairs. Bubbles were blown in milk, forks were used like drum sticks, and yes, each kid burped at the table. A lot!

It.

Was.

Awesome!

A couple years later, we received an invitation to a different kind of dinner. When the kids wrote letters to different world leaders, one of the responses was from a real prince! He lived with his wife, who was a princess, in a country that was named after their family. The prince and princess had children of their own, and they were princes and princesses too!

The prince and princess invited our family over for dinner

at their house, which we secretly hoped would be a castle. Even though the family lived far away across the ocean, we went. It turned out that the prince and his family didn't actually live in a castle, but their dining room table was very fancy— the kind you would expect a prince and princess to eat their dinner at. The table was very long and had wooden legs with carved claw feet on them. Dozens of sparkly glasses lined the top of the table. Candles—perhaps every candle ever made— glowed brightly all around the room. Loads of fancy silverware were placed at every seat. The princess pushed a button by her plate, and a butler arrived with the food. *This is great!* I thought to myself. *We've been practicing our manners for just this kind of thing!*

One of my kids (Adam will remain nameless) tried to cut his chicken, but instead of cutting it, he accidentally launched it off his plate like a hockey puck and sent it flying across the table. It landed with a *thud* right by the prince's plate. There was a long moment of stunned silence. We were all horrified and wondered if the prince's country would think we'd just attacked it—with a piece of chicken!

The prince stared at the chicken by his plate. Then he looked up, and a huge smile spread across his face. He lifted up his fork, positioned it behind the piece of chicken, and asked with a laugh, "Is this a game you play in your country? Shall I launch it back to you?" It was No-Manners Night all over again, only this time it was the royal-family edition! What started as a fancy, serious dinner became a room full of laughter and great conversations about life and relationships, and we made some wonderful new friends.

Something our family has learned over the years is that whether you are having Good-Manners Night or No-Manners Night, making time to sit at a table with new and old friends is important. It's something Jesus spent a lot of time doing too. In fact, did you know that Jesus had His own kind of No-Manners Night? He invited His friends to dinner one evening, and before the dinner started, Jesus got out a bowl of water and a towel and started *washing His friends' feet*. In those days, this broke all kinds of rules about manners, because it was only polite for servants to wash people's feet. The disciples were shocked. Jesus was a Prince who had a lot in common with the prince we met on our trip. He knew that loving people sometimes included welcoming their silly manners, flying chicken, and dirty feet at your table.

After Jesus went back to heaven, His friends continued to meet around tables just like the one you probably have at home. They broke bread together, which means they made sure everyone got a piece, and they shared everything they owned with each other. Isn't that neat? Jesus invites us to our tables every night to do the same. When we gather together with other people, sometimes they break the rules and offend us or hurt our feelings. But do you know what Jesus does when that happens? He invites them back to the table all over again, and we get to invite them back too. Because after all, what Jesus really wants most from us isn't our best manners. He wants us to be good friends with Him and good friends with one another, showing love in ways that break all the normal rules.

15

BEARS

Do you ever peek out your window first thing in the morning to check if there's something interesting outside, like a butterfly or snow or puffy clouds? I did that one morning, and guess what I saw. A huge bear!

Many years ago, our family built a log cabin up in Canada. It's in a beautiful place, located more than a hundred miles away from the nearest roads or cities. I'm not kidding—you can only get there by boat or seaplane (an airplane that can land on water)! We grow vegetables in the garden, catch our food in the ocean, and even make our own electricity from a river. It's a great place for people to live, but it's also a great place for bears. The forest is full of them! Most of the time, the bears stay far away from our cabin because we're so noisy. Sometimes, though, they stroll across our porch and peek into our windows. I guess they're as curious about us as we are about them.

When I was nose-to-nose with that bear through the window, I got really scared. But I held my ground, clapped my hands, waved my arms over my head, and made lots of noise. Do you know what that bear did? He ran away so fast it was like he was never there. All I saw was a blur of legs and fur and ears, running away from me and up the mountain.

When my kids wrote to world leaders and asked to meet with them, the whole family got the chance to visit a country that the United States had once fought against in a war. Both countries used to be very afraid of each other. But that didn't stop my kids from writing a letter to their leader, and it didn't stop our new friend from meeting with us!

We found the leader in a great big building with lots of flags and soldiers standing guard both inside and out. When we arrived at his office, our new friend walked into the room

and shook hands with Lindsey, Richard, and Adam. As we sat down, he looked across the table and confessed with a smile, "I need to tell you children a secret." The kids all leaned forward as he lowered his voice and looked around the room to make sure no one else was listening.

"Whenever I meet with other leaders, I get a little nervous. However, I'm feeling more nervous to meet you today than I feel when I meet with the president of the United States!" Then, with a twinkle in his eye, the leader continued, "When I get nervous, I get really hungry—so let's eat!" He clapped his hands, and into the room marched six waiters wearing white gloves and carrying silver trays filled with candy, cookies, ice cream, and apple juice.

As they sat around his desk sharing candy together, the kids asked the leader what message of hope he would want to share with children around the world. He sat back in his chair and thought for a moment. Then, with the tone of a trusted friend, he said, "Let me tell you another secret. When I was young, my family went camping in the forest. My father would pretend to forget his hat in the woods and would tell me to find it and bring it to him. He was teaching me to face my fears." He leaned in toward the kids a little further and whispered, "This is the part you can't tell anyone: while I walked through the woods, I would whistle to myself because I was scared of running into a bear!" The kids all giggled and promised they wouldn't tell. (I just told you, but you need to promise not to tell anyone else, okay?)

The leader continued, "Here is the message of hope I would give to children around the world: Sometimes it feels like there are a lot of bears in the world—you know, the scary things we have to face. But I want you to know that to make a friend, you must first be a friend. And when you have friends, you don't have to be scared of the bears anymore."

What our new friend reminded us is that we all have been scared of something at one time or another. It's something we all have in common. I think Jesus probably knew what it was like to be scared too. At one point, people came to capture Him with swords. He knew His time on Earth was ending. Even when He should have been the most scared, though, He seemed to be the most confident. I think I know why. It was because God was His Friend and His Father.

The Bible tells us that Jesus kept reminding His friends not to be afraid.

Jesus told them that He would never leave them and that He would even send a helper, the Spirit, to be with them. The Spirit would keep them company, comfort them, give them advice, and make them brave too. Jesus promises the same thing to all of us. Isn't that great? We are Jesus' friends too, and He promises to never leave us either.

No matter what happens, we don't have to be scared anymore. Jesus knows all about the things that scare us, but even when we feel a little scared, we can remember that He's our friend and He's not scared at all. Sure, we'll bump into "bears" now and then. They might be the big, furry kind with teeth, like the one that peeked in my cabin window, or they could be things you're trying to learn how to do for the first time. Whatever your bears look like, remember that you don't ever have to be scared when you face them because you are never alone. Knowing Jesus is with you, you can hold your ground, wave your arms, make lots of noise like I did, and watch your fears run away in a blur of legs and fur and ears like they were never even there.

16

KEYS

When our family got ready to meet with the world leaders after writing them letters, we decided to bring along a really nice present to give to each of them. The problem was, we couldn't think of a good present for someone who leads a whole country. They already have everything—they have a *whole country*. Besides, what did three kids from San Diego have to offer that they might want?

Suddenly, Sweet Maria had an idea. "What if we give them a copy of our house key?"

We all knew that only our most trusted friends had a copy of the key to our house. (And really, those are the only people who *should* have a key to your house!) We wanted our new friends to know that they were welcome and trusted, even though we were from different parts of the world.

Before we left to meet our new friends, we made fifty copies of our house key, and we put them in little boxes. At the end of each interview, we would pray for the leader, and then one of the kids would say, "We brought you a present! This is a copy of our house key. We want you to know that we think of you as our friend, and you are welcome to come to our house anytime. Just bring your key. You can let yourself in!"

Do you know what happened when the kids gave a key to

a president or prime minister or ambassador? Our new friends got tears in their eyes. Every. Single. Time. They always asked the same things: "You trust me with the key to your home? You really want me to come and visit you?"

Some people might think it's not very safe to hand out lots of copies of your house key. It's true that you should only give them to friends, with your parents' permission. What we've learned, though, is that we aren't less secure when we have more friends; we're more secure.

Before Jesus left to go back to heaven, He promised His disciples, "I am going to prepare a home for you!" Heaven is our real home. And our family decided that one of the things we want to do on Earth is to give people a glimpse of heaven. We want them to experience being welcomed into a home the way Jesus welcomes us into His. Jesus is making a home for us, so we get to be part of making a home for others. Opening up our home to friends all over the world has taught us that real friendship means that we love everybody all the time, just as they are, and that everyone is welcome.

Some of our friends in leadership have gone through hard times over the years, and the kids have written them more letters saying, "Remember your key? Come and use it anytime. We're your friends no matter what."

Over the years, we've seen how friendships come to life when people know they are truly welcomed. The world will know what we really believe when they see the way that we love others. If we believe that our home is in heaven, then we can show people that they are welcome at our homes here on Earth.

17

MAKING FRIENDS

Lindsey ran through the doorway after school, dropped her backpack on the floor, and headed upstairs to the computer. The kids were in the habit of checking Lindsey's e-mail every day; they used her account to keep in touch with the new friends we made on our trip to meet with world leaders. We gave each leader a house key and told them that we would have a guest room ready just for them. This was true, but the whole truth was that our "guest room" was really our garage with a couple of bunk beds in it.

Usually, the e-mails that came in simply said hello or asked the kids what they were learning about in school, but this day was different. An ambassador from another country wrote,

Dear Lindsey, Richard, and Adam,
I would like to use my key and visit you in San Diego
with my wife and son. Can we come stay with you?
        Your friend,
        Jaime

"Um, Mom?" Lindsey yelled down the stairs.

"Yeah, honey?"

"I just got an e-mail from an ambassador. He wants to come with his family to stay with us in the garage!"

The kids were all thrilled that an ambassador and his

family were coming to visit, but Sweet Maria was mortified. "We are going to make an ambassador sleep in our *garage*?!" We thought for a moment of all of the things we would need to do to make our house nice enough for the ambassador and his family. Really, all we had to offer were a stack of paper plates and our friendship. Deep down, we all knew that was enough.

We didn't know what to expect when the ambassador and his family arrived. We imagined them pulling up to our

house in a huge stretch limo, with flags and maybe a band, and secret agents would slide down the sides of our house on ropes, talking into their sleeves with little squiggly walkie-talkie earpieces.

Much to our surprise, the ambassador and his family pulled up to our house in a rented minivan. It didn't have flags or anything. I'll be honest: I was a little disappointed when I didn't spot a single secret agent in the bushes by our front door. We greeted the ambassador and his family with warm hugs, and it felt exactly like some old family friends had come to visit. Do you know why? It's because that's exactly what had happened.

Later that evening, after a big dinner of pizza (served on paper plates, of course), we sat on the porch with the ambassador and his family, all happy and full. I couldn't hold back my question any longer.

"Jaime," I said, "we just have to ask: What made you say yes when we asked if you would be our friend and invited you to come visit us?"

The ambassador laughed and then thoughtfully replied, "Well, I get lots of letters every day. Hundreds of letters, actually. I have been an ambassador for years, but never once in all those letters have I heard from any other kids who simply wanted to be friends with me and my family, let alone invite us to their house! When I saw that, how could I say no?"

Our family learned a lot about Jesus from Jaime and his family that day and in the years that followed, as our friendship continued to grow. Jaime didn't want to meet with our kids because they were powerful or rich—he met with them because they simply wanted to be friends. In the same way, Jesus loves welcoming us to spend time with Him, and we can come exactly as we are, because we're His. We don't have to be powerful or rich or anything else to be friends with Jesus.

The way we met the ambassador reminds me of the story about how Zacchaeus met Jesus. When Zacchaeus heard that Jesus was about to walk through his town, he climbed a tree to get a better look over the crowd. Jesus looked up, saw Zacchaeus in the tree, and said, "Zacchaeus, I'm coming over to your house for dinner tonight!" Can you imagine how surprised Zacchaeus must have been? Maybe he wondered if his home would be nice enough. Jesus' friends were surprised too. They knew who Zacchaeus was, and nobody liked him because he wasn't nice to people. Zacchaeus had a habit of taking things that didn't belong to him.

Zacchaeus was stunned that Jesus wanted to have dinner with him, just like my family was surprised when the ambassador wanted to stay at our house. Just like us, Zacchaeus probably didn't know what to expect when his guest arrived, and he may have worried about what Jesus would think once He got to know Zacchaeus more. But after that one visit from Jesus, Zacchaeus walked away changed. He promised that he would return everything he had taken from other people—in fact, he said that he would give back four times more than what he took!

What the kids and I learned from the ambassador, Jesus, and Zacchaeus is this: there is incredible power in loving people, regardless of their status and reputation. We would have missed out on a special friendship if we had decided not to invite the ambassador over because we thought he was too important or that we were too unimportant. Instead of worrying about whether or not we have enough to offer to others, we can trust that offering the best we have, even if it isn't perfect, is enough. God wants to know each of us, and He wants us to know each other.

(18)

EVERYBODY'S IN

When my kids were little, we went through a go-kart building phase. We built little cars using wood, trash cans, wheels, rope, and horns that we found. The go-karts didn't have engines, but luckily, our house is on a street with a small hill. With a good push, they could really get going! As you might

guess, we held lots of races with all the neighbor kids. Soon the block was filled with go-karts. All the kids wanted one!

One day we had an idea: *What if we put all of our little cars in a line and had a parade on our street?* We decided that New Year's Day would be a fun time to have a parade, so we got three hundred balloons and three hundred donuts and invited all our neighbors to come. We told everyone to meet us at the top of the hill at ten o'clock in the morning. A few minutes before ten, there was no one in sight, and we were a little sad that no one was going to join us.

Then, something amazing happened. People started coming out of their houses! Dogs were decorated with bandanas, kids hung streamers from their bikes, and people started tying balloons to cars. To our amazement, a man with a bagpipe arrived a minute before the parade started, and so did a fire engine! Everyone got in line with their dogs, go-karts, and bicycles. Someone yelled, "Go!" and we paraded down the street. Within a minute or two, the parade was over, and everyone was in our front yard eating donuts.

Do you know what the best part of the parade was? No one watched the parade, because everyone was in it. Isn't that great? The curbs were completely empty!

The parade became an annual tradition on our street, and we've held it for twenty-four years so far. Even if we were on the other side of the world, we would figure out how to get back to our neighbors every year for the parade. The only things that have changed are that my kids are taller and now we blow up one thousand balloons. (Three hundred just wasn't enough, but I know I don't need to tell you that.) Year after year, the curbs are still empty!

While I love donuts, balloons, and fire engines, those really aren't what make the parade so special; instead, it's the people who are in it. Each year we ask different neighbors to be the queen or the grand marshal. God wants us to love everyone, but in particular He wants us to love widows, orphans, and

our neighbors. Usually, the women we ask to be the queen have been a part of the neighborhood for years. Some have had hard years or lost their husbands. One year, our mailman was the grand marshal, and another year we asked our little friend Charlie to lead the parade down the street. The parade helps us do a whimsical, joy-filled version of loving everybody. And all it took were some balloons and a box of donuts.

I'm not sure if God picked out exactly who our neighbors would be when we moved onto our street, but I bet He couldn't wait to see how we would love the people living right next to us. When Jesus taught His disciples to love their neighbors, I think He meant exactly that—He wanted them to love the person on the other side of the wall or fence or street. When you love the people living around you, you can bring a lot of hope and joy to neighbors who have been through some very hard things.

What are some joyful ways that you can love your neighbors? Why not start a parade where you live? If you don't have a street in front of your house, make the parade route down the hallways of your apartment building or through a nearby park. Let everybody know there's just one rule: nobody can just watch, and everybody has to be in it!

19

THE GOOD DOCTOR

My kids didn't like going to the doctor when they were growing up. A trip to the doctor's office usually included getting shots and taking medicine that tasted bad. But their attitudes changed when we became friends with a doctor and his wife who lived down the street from us.

The doctor spent his days helping people who were hurt while playing sports. Having a friend with these skills really helped our family because it seemed like every other day the kids got hurt while they were playing. When they did, our friend was always the first person we called for help. He would grab his leather bag, a stethoscope, and some bandages and walk over to our house. When the doctor walked in the door, the whole family knew everything would be better.

One evening, we were sitting at the table eating supper when Adam picked up a dinner roll. He wasn't paying attention, and as he cut through the roll with a knife, Adam ended up cutting into his finger! It was a deep cut, and Sweet Maria and I thought we might need to take Adam to the hospital to get stitches. We called our friend to ask his opinion, and he said, "Hold on a second. I'll be right over."

The doctor put a few things in his leather bag and strolled the three doors down to our house. Within two minutes, he

knocked on our door. He pulled up an empty chair at the dinner table, took out a needle and some thread, and quickly stitched up Adam's finger while chatting with the rest of the family. Less than ten minutes after getting his injury, Adam was all patched up, and we were back to laughing around the table. Can you believe that?

I was so impressed by the doctor's ability to fix the cut on Adam's hand that I asked him to teach me how to do my own stitches. He got a couple of orange peels and demonstrated how to sew the two pieces together. I was fascinated and stitched up every orange in the house. Each time, I'd show the kids how good I was at sewing. The funny thing was, once I learned how to do my own stitches, there were no more cuts in the family. I guess no one wanted to look like those orange peels.

One of the reasons our doctor friend was so special to our family is that he was available to us whenever we needed help. He never seemed bothered or annoyed that we were hurt and needed him. Instead, he just made his way to our side to offer what we needed the most. Jesus does the same. He is always close by, and He delights when we ask Him to help us with our biggest hurts.

The Bible says that Jesus is like a physician. Many people wanted to spend time with Jesus, including the most important and popular people. Jesus didn't spend much time with them, though. He mostly hung out with the people who were sick or who made mistakes. He told His friends, "I didn't come to spend time with people who are healthy. I came to spend time with people who are sick!"

If you've been cut or bruised or if your feelings have been hurt, Jesus is like a doctor who lives on your block—He's nearby if you need Him. Just call His name and He'll come to you, sit at your table, and heal you in ways only He can.

20

THE TOWN

A line of trees in our backyard runs from the corner of our house down the side of the property. I could never figure out what kind of trees they were, but the kids always called them "paper trees" because the bark looks like paper and peels off in sheets. The kids made official-looking property deeds from the bark paper, and each took ownership of his or her own tree. They eventually drew up plans for a whole town in our backyard. There was a jail, a hospital, and a post office. It had everything.

The kids transformed the paper trees into elaborate tree houses. To anyone else, the construction would have looked like a mess of broken wood, pieces of cardboard, and nails, but to the kids, those trees were practically castles. Some of the trees were made into homes; others became stores. The town jail (which looked a lot like our chicken coop) was next to the public square where big announcements could be made. Whenever neighborhood kids came over to play, the kids would give them their own tree to live in. The kids' town was a place where everyone was welcome.

The kids spent hours creating their town and made their own town rules. As the oldest, Lindsey was the self-appointed mayor and resident artist. Richard declared himself the sheriff.

He promised he'd be tough on crime. This left Adam with the role of being the only regular townsperson. Richard didn't have much to do, so he'd arrest Adam once or twice a day and put him in the chicken coop jail.

I learned a lot from my kids as I watched them play. If someone in their town ran out of money, they just grabbed some bark paper and made more. New laws were created—and changed, if necessary—so each person's needs were met. Everyone had a home, food, and the support of their community. The kids even made a town newspaper and circulated what they thought was important news in their world. Headlines like "Richard Passes His Spelling Test" and "Adam Learns to Ride His Bike" were common. They celebrated everyone in the town.

When Jesus was with His disciples, He talked about building a new kind of town here on Earth. It wouldn't be one that was built in trees or in chicken coops; instead, it would be a kingdom built inside of our hearts. Jesus said God was creating a new way to live, and one of the rules in this town was that everyone's needs were supposed to be met. He didn't need any sheriffs or mayors, but He did want people who would help each other out.

God's kingdom seems a lot like the kids' town—a place where old rules don't apply, where there is always enough to go around, and where everyone has a home. As friends of Jesus, we get to be members of His kingdom on Earth, and we get to live by new rules too. God has given each of us a tree in the kingdom. What are you going to make yours look like?

21
PACK LIGHT

Sweet Maria could tell that our kids were up to something. The kids called her into the living room to make an announcement.

"Mom," Richard began in a confident, excited voice, "we've decided to run away from home. We're going on an adventure together!"

Leaving home is a serious part of growing up, but it usually happens after kids are old enough to drive themselves to the store to buy their own fruit snacks. At the time, the kids were ages seven, five, and three—not quite old enough to leave home! With their siblings at their sides, though, our kids decided they were ready to take on the world. There was always the possibility that they might be eaten by a bear or tiger, but the kids weren't too afraid of that.

Matching their sincerity and excitement, Sweet Maria responded, "Can I help you pack?" Sweet Maria could tell that this was one of those important moments of childhood whimsy and adventure.

Richard raided the pantry for dinosaur fruit snacks, Lindsey dug through Sweet Maria's side of the closet looking for scarves, and Adam sat on the floor of the bathroom, going through a drawer in search of bandages.

The kids set off out the back door, outfitted with a few supplies and a lot of excitement. They had sticks over their shoulders with bundles tied to the ends, bulging under the weight of fruit snacks and bandages.

The Goff kids' great adventure as runaways began in a front corner of the yard. Their route led them up the side yard, along the back wall, around the garage, and up to the other front corner of the yard. Somewhere along the route, possibly near the garage, the rations disappeared completely. Richard and Adam looked a little guilty with their cheeks stuffed.

"That's okay," Lindsey said, "We can live off the land!" None of the kids actually knew what it meant to live off the land but figured it had something to do with mud pies. They knew they would have enough, not because they had packed a lot to bring with them, but because they had each other.

By dinnertime, the kids decided they'd had enough of life on the road and came back inside. They'd had a great day and couldn't wait to share their experience with Sweet Maria and me.

Jesus often reminded His friends not to worry about things like clothes and food when they went on their adventures, because they had a Father in heaven who would take care of those things. What I learned from watching Lindsey, Richard, and Adam's brief life on the road (well, in our backyard) was that they didn't need those things either. Instead, they needed things like courage and kindness and curiosity. The kids weren't afraid to leave home because they had each other. We don't have to be afraid when we go on adventures either. Trust God, go with people you love, and follow where Jesus leads you.

22

THE JEEP

I've always thought Jeeps are the coolest cars ever made. They're tough and fun, and I especially like the ones that don't have a roof. I used to have a bright red Jeep, and it ended up helping me learn a very important lesson.

A few years ago, I was driving home from church. Out of nowhere, another car drove toward me from a side street and crashed into the driver's side of my Jeep. Before I knew what had happened, my car flipped over, and I went flying right out of the roof! I knew that I was always supposed to wear my seatbelt, but this time I had forgotten. That was a really big mistake.

I landed in a sitting position on the asphalt, facing my wrecked car. Pieces of the Jeep were scattered everywhere—in the street, on a lawn, and even lodged in a nearby fence. It was a mess! I checked to see if I was okay.

Do I have all my arms and legs? Check.

Fingers and toes? Check.

Slowly, I stood up and realized that I felt just fine. I walked over to the car that had just hit me. The stunned driver was sitting behind her steering wheel, holding on for dear life, eyes staring forward. Her knuckles were white.

I popped my head in her window. "Hi! I'm Bob. What's your name?"

The driver was at least ninety years old, small, fragile, and scared. It took her a moment to respond. "I . . . I'm Lynn," she stuttered.

"Lynn, are you okay?" I asked.

"I . . . think so," she said. Suddenly, tears came to her eyes. "I'm so sorry . . . Did you know you flew out of your roof?!"

"Oh, Lynn," I said, matching her serious tone but with a smile in my voice. "I can't lie. That was a pretty big surprise, but luckily I'm okay. So really, no worries at all. Everything's great!"

Lynn still felt terrible, but of course I forgave her on the spot. It really had been an amazing ride.

A few days later, I received a phone call. It was Lynn. "I'm *so sorry*, Bob," she said in a tearful voice.

"Oh, Lynn," I said, "really, don't worry about it. You are totally forgiven. I'm great! Not even a bruise. No need to call again."

The funny thing is, she *didn't* stop calling. Over the next few days, I got daily phone calls from Lynn. Each time, she would apologize, and I would remind her that everything was okay. For some reason, she just didn't believe me when I said that she was forgiven.

Jesus talked a lot about forgiving people. Do you know how many times Jesus wants you to forgive someone who has done something wrong to you? Think of the biggest number you can imagine and add a couple more zeros at the end, and then maybe you'd be close to the number of times you need to forgive someone. Jesus wants us to *always* forgive others.

But maybe you know what it feels like to be Lynn, and you feel awful for making a mistake. Maybe you don't believe people when they say you're forgiven. Sometimes we need to *see* that we are forgiven, instead of only hearing the words.

So I hatched a plan. On the fifth day Lynn called to tell me she was sorry, I called up a florist and ordered a huge bouquet of flowers. I included a card that said, "Dear Lynn, it was nice running into you the other day. You don't need to call anymore! Love, Bob."

Love and forgiveness carry the most weight when they are *done*, rather than simply said. That's why it was so important that Jesus came. God didn't just *tell* us we were forgiven; He sent Jesus to be with us and *show* us that we are forgiven.

I've seen Lynn a few times since the accident. It took a while, but I think she really believes she's forgiven. I think God's hoping we'll feel the same way.

23

STAR NIGHT

Jesus said a lot of things that don't really make sense the first time you hear them. They sound upside down and backward. He said things like, "In My kingdom, humble people who put themselves at the back of the line will end up being at the front of the line."

He also said, "If you want to be great, then you must be a servant to those around you."

It was always hard for me to understand how Jesus' rules could be so different from the way everyone else operates.

Someone once told me that you don't really learn something until you teach it to somebody else. When I became a teacher at a college, I learned what Jesus meant when He talked about His backward kingdom because I taught some of these same ideas to my students.

Before I tell you about the college students, though, I have to tell you about a tradition we have in our family. When our kids were growing up, Sweet Maria and I made up a dinner game we called "Star Night." Star Night really just started out as a way to get our kids to eat their vegetables, but don't tell them that! On Star Night, Sweet Maria would serve dinner on paper plates. Before dishing up the kids' dinners, she would draw a star on the bottom of one of the plates. When

the kids finished eating everything on their plates (including their veggies!), they got to peek underneath to see if they had the star. Whoever had the star got to choose the dessert for the whole family.

The kids loved Star Night, and Sweet Maria and I did too because it made something as ordinary as eating broccoli a lot more fun.

When I started teaching college, I decided to share the Star Night tradition with my students by making a "Star Test." Before each test, I would draw a star on the back of one of the papers. Whoever found the star on the back of their test could ask me for the answer to one of the questions on the exam, and I would write the answer on the board for everyone to see. My tests have lots of questions, and they're really difficult, so the students liked knowing they'd get at least one of the hard questions correct.

The students loved the Star Test, and I did too because it made something as ordinary as taking a test a lot more fun.

What my students didn't know, though, is that I wanted to teach them something even more important than the answers to the test questions. That's why I gave the students a choice—if they found a star on the back of their test, they could ask for the answer to any question, like I said before, or they could give their star away and let someone else pick the question. What the students didn't know is that if someone gave the star away to someone else, he or she wouldn't just get one answer right; I would give the student a perfect score on the *whole test*.

One of the other backward-sounding things Jesus taught is that we can find our lives if we give them up to follow Him. Following Jesus and His teachings is a little like giving up the star question and then finding out that you got a perfect score on the whole test. If we give up our little dreams for our lives, we get Jesus' big dreams and plans instead—and they're much, much better.

For ten years, I passed out tests on test days and let the student with the star either ask for an answer to a question or give the star away to someone else. During those ten years, every single star student chose to keep the star and ask a question. I wasn't upset with them for using the star themselves, but each time I secretly hoped they would give it away instead.

One day, after I passed out the tests, a girl with the star on her test raised her hand. As always, I asked if she would rather get the answer to one of her questions or give the star away. The girl was quiet for a moment, and then she said, "You know, I think I'll give it away."

I could hardly hide my excitement as I waited to tell the girl the news—she was going to get a perfect score on her test! While the students finished up their exams, I opened my computer and checked the girl's grades. As it turns out, she was struggling in my class. Her other test scores weren't very good. She was the student who probably needed a free answer most of all, but she still gave away the star to help someone else. I realized that this is exactly what Jesus was talking about.

By putting the needs of someone else above her own needs, the girl modeled the kind of backward kingdom Jesus talked about. It was only later that she discovered the only way to have it all was to give away what she had.

(24)

RESTORE KIDS

Some of the greatest leaders and teachers I know are about your age, and they live in a town in Northern Uganda called Gulu.

Uganda, a country in Africa, had a civil war that lasted for many years. A civil war is when the people within a single country fight against each other. People from the northern part of the country were angry with people from the southern part of the country, and Gulu was a tiny town caught in the middle. Sadly, many kids in Gulu were affected and hurt by this war.

The war is over now, but many kids missed out on school during those years of fighting. They needed help getting caught up but couldn't afford the school fees. When I learned about this, I had an idea: What better way to help a country recover from a war than to start a school?

We decided that this wouldn't be just any school; it would be a *leadership* school. Kids who went to this school would learn about Jesus and learn how to lead in the backward way that Jesus taught. Jesus said that real leaders love their enemies, serve the poor, and treat others the way they want to be treated. The type of leadership Jesus taught about is hard, but it can change everything. We decided to call the school

Restore Academy because the word *restore* means to fix things that are broken.

When things go wrong in the world, God cares about making them right. Making things right and fair is called *justice*. Justice means looking out for those who have been hurt and being part of their healing. The thing about justice, though, is that it can't happen without love.

What I've learned from the kids at Restore Academy is that even though they have experienced very hard things, they know a lot about how to love. Many of these kids don't have families anymore because of the war, so the kids at the school are placed into their own family groups. The kids meet in these groups and take care of each other. They listen to and support each other, and they have become each other's families. Through their love for each other, these kids are setting right the things that went wrong in their country. They are living out lives of justice.

It's easy to think that bringing justice to the world is something only grown-ups can do, and the truth is a lot of grown-ups are working very hard to love others and make things right in the world. What I want you to know, though, is that *every time* you forgive someone who has hurt you or go out of your way to serve someone who needs help or stand up for someone who is being picked on or share what you have with someone who has less than you, you are helping to heal the world. Kids like you and the kids at the Restore Academy are becoming love and bringing justice to the world.

25

FREEING SLAVES

During His life, Jesus did some amazing things. He performed miracles and healed many people. He walked on water once, and He fed dinner to five thousand people. There weren't even any dishes to clean afterward. Can you believe that?

Do you know what Jesus spent most of His time doing, though? He spent His days teaching people how to please God. Jesus taught so many lessons that people started calling Him "Teacher."

Whenever Jesus traveled to a new town, people would come running to see the Teacher from Nazareth they had heard so much about. When Jesus saw the crowds, the Bible says that He had *compassion* on them. They were curious or excited or nervous or afraid, and Jesus would gather the people around and explain to them the new kind of life God had planned for them. This new kind of life was all about giving to others, being humble, and being nice to people who are mean to you—things that are hard for most of us.

During these talks, some people would ask Jesus questions just to see if they could trick Him. They wanted to get Him in trouble. A few of these tricksters were lawyers.

Lawyers are people who help folks figure out what laws

mean, and they help enforce those laws. This isn't a bad thing. In fact, it can be a really good thing when it's done well. But when good things are used in the wrong way, they aren't that great anymore. Jesus spoke to the lawyers in the crowd and said, "Listen! You people who teach laws are worried more about the laws themselves than about the *people* the laws are supposed to guide and protect. If you want to follow Me, that has to stop."

The words Jesus said to the lawyers always struck home with me because, you see, *I am a lawyer.* I help people figure out laws and how to enforce them. I'm not embarrassed about being a lawyer. I love being a lawyer! I realized that if I were going to be a lawyer and follow Jesus too, I would need to be the kind of lawyer who really helps people.

I learned that there are many lawyers who also love Jesus and are trying to help people the way He said we should. I met with some of these lawyers, and we went to other countries to work with judges and police officers and government leaders to help them catch bad guys who were hurting people. This changed the way I did my job forever.

I remember one hot, dark night in a village in rural India. We were hiding on the rooftop of an old building with some small, flickering candles providing our only light. Some people in this village were being held as slaves, which means that other people broke the law and made them work without paying them in return. We planned a secret meeting with the slaves on the rooftop, and one by one people began to sneak up onto the roof. The other lawyers and I recorded their stories and took fingerprints and pictures, gathering evidence for the police.

Those few hours we spent collecting stories gave the police enough information to capture the people who were holding our new friends in slavery. The slave owners went to jail. The slaves were set free.

I saw how being a lawyer could really help people in desperate need. This ruined my career as a lawyer in the best kind of way. I came home from that trip and immediately quit my job at the big law firm I was working for. I started a new law firm with a friend who cared about justice just like I did. We continued to do normal "lawyer" kinds of things, but at the same time, we started doing things for people in other countries who had been made slaves, had things taken from them, or who were thrown in jail unfairly.

Following Jesus isn't easy; it costs us something. But that doesn't mean it will cost everyone the same thing. For me, following Jesus cost me a job working as a normal lawyer. Maybe following Jesus will cost you something different than it costs one of your friends. Don't worry about it. Figure out who God wants you to be and then do what it takes to become that person.

I haven't been a normal lawyer since that first trip to India, and it's been terrific. I had to give up being normal. Maybe you will too. When we follow Jesus, we stop settling for normal and typical anymore. Instead, we get to give away tremendous amounts of love with tremendous amounts of courage, even if it means doing our jobs a little differently than most people would expect.

26

FINDING ROCK

As I mentioned earlier, our family built a cabin up in Canada next to a Young Life camp. It's a beautiful place, with tall mountains and wide inlets and rushing waterfalls of freezing-cold glacier water. The problem with building a cabin there is that the land is very steep, covered in trees, and difficult to get to.

We first drew a picture of what we wanted the house to look like, but then we needed to make a big, flat spot for the house to sit on. You might be wondering how we made a flat spot out of the steep mountainside covered in loose dirt and big boulders. Guess what. We had to use dynamite to blast the dirt and rock away!

I always thought dynamite would work the way it does in the movies, with an exciting trail of flames racing down a long string attached to the dynamite—and then a huge explosion! It doesn't always work that way, though. Sometimes, after the fuse is lit and everyone hides behind rocks, the trail of flames fizzles out. When that happened to us, we all looked at each other, wondering who would check to see if the flame went out a hundred feet from the dynamite or just two inches.

Eventually, someone got up the courage to tiptoe back to the fuse, relight it, and run for cover again. After the dust

settled from the explosion, do you know what we found buried under all of the dirt and moss and loose stones? Solid rock. This is what we wanted to build our house on.

Jesus was a carpenter, so when He talked about building houses, people listened to Him. One time, Jesus told a story of two different men who built houses. One man built his house on loose sand, but when the wind and rain came, the house washed away because it didn't have a strong foundation under it. The other man, though, built his house on solid rock, and when the wind and rain came, the house stayed put. Jesus told stories like that to teach us bigger lessons about how God wants us to live.

God wants us to build everything in our lives on solid rock. Not all of the things we'll build will be houses to live in. In fact, most won't be buildings at all. We'll build our families, friendships, and communities, and a solid foundation for those will be all the things Jesus taught us about—things like love, forgiveness, and grace. Sometimes it takes a little blasting in our lives to get down to the stuff we can build on. We'll need to clear away things like selfishness and impatience. You won't need dynamite to do this, though. You may just need a friend to help you.

I'm sure you have dreams and plans about things you'd like to build too. The lesson I learned from Jesus is that the things we create are only as good as the foundations they are built on. When you make your life about the things that matter most—loving God and loving others—you'll have a solid foundation for building everything else in your life.

27

LIVING WATER

Do you remember the cabin in Canada I told you about before? Our family calls it the Lodge. One of my favorite things about the Lodge is that it has been a safe place for people to solve problems.

Jesus gave some great ideas on how we could solve problems. He said that if we have a problem with someone else, we need to go to that person directly and talk about it so we can be friends again. Sometimes talking through a problem can be hard, and we might need to ask someone else to help us. Jesus said that was okay too. An important part of loving others is giving them the chance to make things right when they've made a mistake. If you've made a mistake and need someone to help you talk it through, that's something parents and teachers are *really* good at. When Jesus didn't know what to do, He asked His Father for help. We can do the same.

When our family made friends with different world leaders, we found out that some of the countries weren't getting along very well. There had been wars, and people had said unkind things, so the leaders had trouble talking to each other. We had just built the Lodge, so we thought, *What could be a better place to bring together people who are having a hard time talking to each other? Maybe we could help them become friends.*

For the first gathering at the Lodge, we invited folks from five different countries that were *very* upset with each other. We didn't tell them beforehand who else we had invited. We thought they might not come if they knew! When they all arrived, it was a little awkward. Our new friends were shocked. "You want *me* to spend time with *them*?!" they each exclaimed, pointing to someone in the room they didn't like. "That person's country is at *war* with my country! We can't be *friends*!"

Our new friends hadn't been at the Lodge for long before they raised their voices and starting saying mean things to each other. It was getting bad fast, and I could tell that our new friends needed help getting past these problems.

"Friends," I said, stopping the fight. "In our house, we have a rule: anyone who fights has to jump off the cliff behind the Lodge into the water with me. Let's go."

There was a brief moment of stunned silence, but they could see I was serious. One by one, our guests made the leap into the freezing cold water with all their clothes on. Something amazing happened as we all bobbed in the salty ocean water. The fights were forgotten, and our new friends started cheering each other on to jump again. They laughed until their sides hurt. People climbed up the cliff to do more jumps. Some people jumped together, holding hands to help each other conquer their fear of heights. This shared moment of bravery, whimsy, and adventure put conflict in its rightful place—the bottom of the ocean. The water dissolved the anger the leaders had toward each other. That evening, after an afternoon of cliff jumping, these new friends, who had been angry with each other just a few hours before, sat in a circle and shared stories and talked about their hopes for the future of their countries.

I'm not surprised that Jesus talked about water so much. His first miracle was changing ordinary water into wine. He walked on water, was baptized in it, and calmed it when the waves got big. He even compared Himself to water, saying that the life He had come to bring was so good for us it would be like taking a drink of water and never being thirsty again.

I think we can do a lot more with water than we think. We may not be able to walk on it, but the next time you have a problem with someone and can't fig-ure out how to solve it, you might want to just jump in the water together! You don't need to jump off a cliff (and, really, you should only do that with permission from a grown-up), but maybe you could think of something else to do to help bring people together!

28

BIBLE DOING

One of my favorite movies of all time is *Hook.* Have you ever seen it? It's the story of Peter Pan, but unlike the cartoon version, it has real-life people playing the characters. In this version of the story, Peter grew up to be a boring lawyer named Peter Banning. When his kids were captured by Captain Hook the pirate, Peter Banning had to go back to Neverland to rescue them. The problem at the beginning of the movie is that Peter forgot who he was. He forgot he was Peter Pan. We all forget who we are at times.

The whole movie is great, but my favorite part is when Peter Banning has dinner with the Lost Boys on his first night back in Neverland. He sits down at the table, smells delicious food, and is ready to dig in. When the Lost Boys remove the lids from the platters, Peter is confused—there's nothing there! All around him he sees the Lost Boys chomping away on seemingly invisible food, and he's confused about why he can't also see the food.

The problem was this: Peter was just watching the Lost Boys eat. Peter needed to *participate* before he could see the food. In order to *believe* the way the Lost Boys did, he had to *do what they did.*

I think that faith can be the same way. In order to believe,

we can't just learn things about Jesus. We need to do things with Him. We need to get to the *do* part. I've met with the same group of guys every Friday morning for over ten years. When we're together, we certainly learn things about Jesus, but we're not there to study Him. Studying is good, but by itself it's just like Peter Banning sitting at the dinner table and not eating a thing. Our faith becomes real when do what we believe.

Instead of a Bible *study*, my friends and I meet every Friday morning to have a Bible *doing*. We read the things that Jesus taught, and then we go out and put them into action in our day-to-day lives. We try to do the big things Jesus talked about and the small ones too. Every time we do the things Jesus talked about instead of just talking about them, something changes in us. It's like we can see the food at the Lost Boys' dinner. Jesus has set that kind of feast in front of us and hopes we'll all be part of it.

One of the things we'll do at the Bible doing is think of ways we can understand our faith better by *doing* something. I'll give you one example. A lot of times, the position of our bodies can affect the position of our hearts and minds. Try this: hold your hands in really tight fists in front of you. Couldn't you get really angry at someone if your fists were clinched? Now try holding your hands palms up, with your fingers stretched out in front of you. It's harder to be angry, isn't it? I've experienced faith to be the same way. When I put faith into action with my body, then my heart and mind follow along.

I don't think Jesus wants us to just agree with Him. I think He wants us to take what He taught His friends and turn it into *action*. When we actually *do* the things that Jesus said— giving food to people who are hungry, being generous with our time and money, or being nice to people who are mean to us— our hearts will follow our actions, and our faith will become real!

29

HUMBLE VOICES CARRY FAR

The house where our family lives is right by the water, and there's something funny about water that most people don't realize—sound carries over it and travels very far. If I were on a boat on one side of a lake and you were on a boat on the other side of a lake and we started hollering at each other, I'd probably be able to hear you as clear as a bell. I don't know the science behind it, but I do know that water is like God's own sound system. In fact, one time when a huge crowd came to hear Jesus speak, He hopped in a boat and preached from the water. I bet it was so they could hear Him better.

Sweet Maria and I will sit on our back porch and listen to whole conversations as people sail past our home on their boats. A lot of times the conversations make me laugh because people talk about funny things without realizing how far and loudly their voices are traveling over the water. Lately, though, they've got me thinking, *I wonder if our voices are actually meant to travel far into other people's lives?*

I have a good friend named Scott, and he's one of those kind, humble people you would drop everything to listen to. You know the kind of person I'm talking about—they don't

make you feel bad if you mess up, and their encouraging words make you feel better. Those humble voices carry far.

Scott is really good at something I'm not very good at: he is an amazing figure skater. I can do trips and flops on ice skates. He can do jumps and flips! On *ice skates*. As a matter of fact, Scott is so good at ice skating that he went to the Olympics and won a gold medal!

There's a lot to like about Scott, but one day, he told me a story of his ice-skating days that only made me like him more. You see, as an Olympian, Scott has done a *lot* of ice-skating competitions, and one of them went horribly wrong. Scott glided across the ice on his skates, jumped, and landed badly. Instead of skating away gracefully, he fell smack on his belly and slid across the ice and into a wall. I know what you're thinking—falling on ice is no fun because it is hard and cold and wet. When Scott stood up, he looked down at himself to make sure he still had his arms and legs, and he saw that his pants were soaking wet. It looked just like he'd had an accident!

Now, if it were me, I probably would have quit then and there, but of course Scott didn't. He got up—wet pants and all—and finished skating. He might not have won first place at that competition, but he didn't let a mistake stop him from finishing what he set out to do. Humble people do that.

Another amazing thing about Scott is that even though he

has a bunch of gold medals, he doesn't brag about them. He doesn't have them sitting out for everyone to look at. If you met Scott, the first thing he would tell you is that he loves his kids. He has four kids of his own, but his love for kids doesn't stop there. Scott and his wife, Tracie, spend their time taking care of families and kids in a country called Haiti. To Scott and Tracie, kids are worth more than all the gold medals in the world.

Scott and Tracie are humble people with voices that carry far in this world, right into the lives of the people they love. They use their voices and their lives to make the world a better place. What are some ways you can use your words to make the world a better place too? When you do, I promise you this: your humble voice will carry far.

30

PLAY BALL

I recently heard a story about a softball game that went horribly wrong, and at the same time, all the important things went right. Let me explain what happened.

The batter stepped up to home plate, squinting against the late afternoon sunlight. The pitcher threw the ball, the batter swung hard, and the bat made a loud *smack!* The ball soared over the center-field fence. It was a home run! The batter started running as fast as she could, racing toward first base. She was thrilled that she had just hit a home run.

When the batter got to first base, though, something went terribly wrong. As she rounded the base, something in her leg popped, and she crumpled to the ground in pain. She tried to get up and run to the next base, but she fell again. She wasn't able to make it on her own, and if she couldn't round all the bases, her team would lose the game. One of the rules in softball is that the runner needs to touch all the bases before touching home plate or the home run doesn't count. Another rule is that a runner's teammates aren't allowed to help her get around the bases. If her teammates helped, the team would get an automatic out and they would lose the game.

The player lay on the ground with hot tears of disappointment filling her eyes. She knew she'd never be able to make

it around the bases on her own, and she was in terrible pain. As she looked up, though, something amazing happened. Two players from the *other team* were walking toward her. Without saying anything, the players gently grabbed hold of her arms and slung them around their shoulders. Everyone in the stands stood speechless as the opposing team members helped the injured player around the bases.

A little bit earlier, I talked about how Jesus' kingdom and the things He taught sometimes seem backward. Jesus said He had a whole new set of rules about how His friends will treat each other. I love the story of the softball players because the girls from the other team decided to lose the game to help someone who was hurt. By giving away their love, they lived out the kind of love Jesus talked about. They laid down their dreams and goals for someone else because they knew that we only truly win at the things that matter in life if we're willing to lose everything.

Jesus talked about winning and losing with His friends. One time, some of His friends argued about who would get to sit in the chairs closest to Jesus in heaven. It seems silly now, but at the time, the disciples didn't understand Jesus' upside-down kingdom. In Jesus' time, whenever people had dinner at someone else's house, the seat everyone wanted was the seat closest to the host of the party. If you got that special seat, it was a way of telling everyone else at the party, "I'm the best!" Jesus told His friends that a different kind of person would be great in His kingdom. He said that people who wanted to be great—the winners—in His kingdom would be the people who helped other people instead of helping themselves.

If you play sports, you probably wear a jersey that shows people which team you're on—and which team you're not on. We're all part of different teams. Sometimes they're sports teams, but they can also look like groups of friends, the neighborhoods we live in, and sometimes even the churches we go to. It's a great feeling to belong to a group of people we love and who love us back.

Followers of Jesus, though, are willing to forget about the jerseys and to love people outside of their own communities because in Jesus' kingdom, everyone is part of the same team. Just like the softball players, we get to spend our lives helping people who have been hurt make it around all the bases.

31

DISNEYLAND

It's no secret that I love Disneyland. If I could, I would go there every day. I love the characters and rides, the cotton candy and balloons, the festive crowds of people, and the Mickey Mouse ears. I even love the fake barrels of dynamite, even though I was a little disappointed when I found out they weren't real. I love a lot of things about Disneyland, but my favorite part of the whole park is Tom Sawyer Island. Tom Sawyer Island is the one place in Disneyland where there aren't any rides. It's just a place to run and jump and dream. Plus, it's got a pirate ship docked next to it. Who wouldn't like a place that comes with a pirate ship?

Another thing I love about Disneyland is the whimsy and creativity that went into filling everything at the park with meaning. Even though it is a huge place, there are lots of little details like ropes and twinkly lights and mountains and vanilla-scented air that somehow make you feel like you're in Switzerland and on a pirate ship and in outer space—all in the same day!

Did you know that Disneyland wasn't always a very fun place to visit? On the first day that the park opened, the water fountains didn't work. It was so hot that the asphalt in the streets kept melting, and women's shoes sunk right into the

ground. The park ran out of food, and some of the rides even broke down. Disneyland was supposed to be the "Happiest Place on Earth," but it was far from it.

To me, the most surprising thing is that the man who made the park, Walt Disney, didn't give up. The park opened again the next day, and the people running Disneyland fixed a few of the things that had gone wrong. They kept opening the park, day by day, and it slowly grew into the amazing place it is today.

As I've grown up, I've found that a lot of my very best plans can turn out just like the opening day of Disneyland. I make mistakes, things don't go as planned, and people get upset. If I gave up after each failure, some of the most special things in my life wouldn't exist today. The same is true for you. If you give up too early, the people around you won't have the chance to see all that God can do through you.

When I read the Bible recently, I noticed something: Jesus told the disciples that they would do greater things than He did because His Spirit would be in them. Jesus never told His friends that things would be easy. Not once. But He did promise that He would never leave them, even when things go wrong. He promises the same thing to us. Isn't that amazing?

When you dream about what you want to do with your life, don't be afraid that things might go wrong. In fact, they probably will at some point. Just remember that we are not our successes or our failures. God delights in our attempts, and He loves walking beside you when you try new things, even if it takes a few tries to get them right.

GO PICK A FIGHT

When I was in middle school, I picked a fight with Dale, the bully at my school. I didn't like Dale because he always pushed the little kids around, and I wasn't scared of him because I was bigger than he was. One day, I had seen enough of Dale's bullying, and I picked a fight with him on the playground after school.

Now, I know I don't need to tell you this because you already understand this so much better than I did as a kid—using fists to pick a fight is definitely a bad idea. Hurting someone else will never solve a problem. It only makes the problem worse! All Dale and I got from the fight were a couple of bloody noses and suspensions from school.

As I grew up and learned about who Jesus was, I realized that Jesus picked some fights too. His fights were different than the fight I picked with Dale, though. Jesus' fights were the right kind. His fights were against the *things* that hurt other people, instead of the people themselves. Jesus' fights created life and joy and peace instead of bloody noses. Over the years, I have made some amazing friends who are picking fights the same way Jesus did. I'll tell you about a few of them.

I have a friend named Jamie who picked a fight against

sadness and loneliness. He spends his life telling people they are loved and that their lives are special to God.

My friend Darla picked a fight against hopelessness. She spends her life telling stories through movies that teach kids to be brave, have confidence in who they are, and believe that they can make the world a better place.

I have a friend named John who picked a fight against slavery. He spends his life searching for people who need to be freed and wants to end slavery during his lifetime.

Another friend named Danielle picked a fight against hunger and poverty in a big city. She gives food and love to people who don't have enough of either.

My friend Mike picked a fight with guilt and shame. He tells people how they can forgive themselves and each other for mistakes they have made.

These are the kinds of fights Jesus wanted His friends to take on. Jesus knew some really sad things would happen in the world. Jesus told His friends over and over again that even when sad things happened, they shouldn't be afraid. He let them know He was bigger than any of those scary things and that He would always be with them.

Your parents and other adults who love you will tell you not to get into fights, and they're right. You weren't made to get in fights that hurt other people. There are other kinds of fights that are worth your time. You'll know them when you see them. When a kid in your class is being picked on or when you notice someone who doesn't have any friends, you get to pick a fight against the loneliness and hurt they are feeling. You could ask them to sit with you at lunch and play with you at recess. Every time we pick the right kind of fight, the world will know a little more about the heart of Jesus.

33

ICE CREAM DROP

It's not a secret that I love seaplanes. Seaplanes take off and land on the water. In a way, they're like pickup trucks because they're built to carry big things like chainsaws and tree stumps and snowmobiles. But unlike pickup trucks, they can fly and float! Seaplanes are built for adventures.

One of my first seaplane adventures was up in Canada with my friend Grant. The Young Life camp I told you about before has a hiking program in the mountains there, and high school kids go on adventures in the mountains and hear about Jesus. The trips last for about six days, and the kids climb mountains that are eight thousand feet tall. It's not an easy hike, but it's even harder if it rains or snows at the top of the mountain.

Our family spends our summers next to the Young Life camp, and one week my friend Grant flew up in his seaplane to visit. It was a cold, drizzly, Pacific Northwest kind of day, and I had heard that a group of high school kids was on a hiking trip in the mountains. They were having a tough time in the cold weather. Some kids were feeling sick, others were worn out, their socks and jackets were wet, and they were ready to be home. But they were still one last push from the top of the mountain. Grant and I listened to the radio that night when

the guides called in to the camp. The hikers were torn between heading for the mountain summit with their unhappy crew or turning back in the morning and calling it a trip. In the end, the guides decided they'd go for the summit in the morning.

Grant and I hatched a plan. We figured if the campers were on the glacier at the top of the mountain, we'd be able to see them from the plane. And if we could see them, we could probably throw something from the plane down to them, couldn't we? We laughed together the next morning as we jumped in the seaplane to fly to the nearest grocery story, one hundred miles away, to get several cases of ice cream sandwiches.

With my kids securely strapped in the plane, we slowly circled up toward the snowcapped summit. When we were finally about a thousand feet over the summit, we scanned the glacier and spotted the hikers moving slowly through the snow, looking like a tiny line of wet, cold ants.

We decided to do a first pass right over the hikers to get their attention. As we flew over their heads, the tired kids all looked up and started waving. Grant made the plane's wings wave back. Then, my kids helped me open a hatch in the bottom of the seaplane. On our second pass over, we dropped ice cream through the hatch and watched it rain down on the trail in front of the hikers. From up above, we saw the tiny dots of hikers break from their line and run to see what had been dropped on the snow nearby. We did a third pass over the field of ice cream sandwiches, and this time we could see the campers jumping up and down, waving at us wildly, letting out whoops of joy we could almost hear over the roar of the plane's huge engine.

What I learned that day from Grant and my kids and the hikers is this: God delights in surprising us. I've found that in my hardest moments, when I feel the most in need of encouragement, I don't hear God's voice talking to me out loud—instead, God sends me a friend to remind me about His tremendous love for me.

The next time you feel discouraged, look up! Look around you! Look beside you! God knows just what you need, and He has already picked people out to encourage you, even if you don't know who they are yet. Do you want to know the extra fun part? God has put *you* in the lives of others to do the same. Take a moment right now and think about the other kids and even the adults in your life who you might be able to encourage. Let God use you to be the surprise He has planned for someone else's life.

34

POPCORN BAGS

When my kids were little, they had trouble keeping track of time. I bet you know what that feels like. Are you ever on long car trips where your parents say you'll be there in twenty-five minutes? It might as well be twenty-five years when you're bored in the back seat of a car.

When my kids were still learning how to track the passage of time, I figured out a way to explain time to them that helped on those long car rides. A favorite snack in our house was popcorn—the kids loved to watch the kernels pop in the microwave. They knew what it felt like to wait for a bag of popcorn and understood how long it took to pop, so I decided to start using popcorn bags as a unit of time in our house. Saying "We'll be home in five minutes" didn't mean much to the kids, so instead I'd say, "We'll be home in two popcorn bags!"

The funny thing is, it totally worked! The kids could imagine two bags of popcorn popping more easily than they could imagine a clock ticking for five minutes, even though those things take the same amount of time. Counting popcorn bags made the long trip home much easier for my kids.

Did you know that Jesus talked a lot about waiting and watching for time to pass? Jesus came to Earth to start a new kingdom, but He said we'll have to wait a while before that

kingdom is finished. Jesus went back to heaven to get our new home ready, but He promised to come back again to finish His kingdom on Earth. The Bible talks about a day when Jesus will make heaven happen *right here on Earth*, and everything that ever went wrong in the world will be made right. Doesn't that sound great?!

Jesus knew that waiting for good things can be hard, just like waiting during a long trip home is hard. So, Jesus gave us a job to do during the waiting. We get to help prepare the Earth for Him to come back! We can do this by befriending people who don't have many friends or by sharing our favorite snack with someone else. Or we can tell people about all the great things God has done. This is a full-time job, and we all get to join in. Jesus said that no one knows how many minutes or hours or days are left until He comes back. There are no bags of popcorn to keep track of. But while we're waiting, we can spend our time loving God and loving others.

When my kids were little, counting bags of popcorn helped them mark the passage of time. While we wait for Jesus, we can do the same thing by filling our days with acts of love and grace. We don't know when Jesus will come back, but we can get things ready for His return.

35

INVITED VS. WELCOME

When I was growing up, my parents taught me to always use good manners. If I ever forgot to say, "Thank you," my parents would prompt me to remember by saying, "You're welcome!"

"Oops!" I would quickly say. "Sorry. Thank you!"

When I grew up, I started spending a lot of time in the country of Uganda. I wanted to have good manners while I was there, so I tried to learn about the different ways that people are polite in Uganda. When I was in Uganda, I always felt like I was in trouble because everywhere I went, from entering the country at the airport to getting in a taxi to going to the grocery store, people would say to me, "You're welcome!" I would feel really bad because I thought that they were reminding me to say "Thank you."

"Oops!" I would say. "Sorry. Thank you!"

I realized later that my new Ugandan friends weren't actually prompting me to have better manners. When they said, "You're welcome," what they meant was *you are welcome here!* These weren't words of correction. They were words of invitation.

Have you ever been invited somewhere but didn't feel very welcome when you got there? Just being invited somewhere is really different from being welcomed, isn't it? It's the difference between someone just being polite to you because they should and someone actually being excited to see you and wanting to spend time with you.

Whenever people come to our home now, I make a point to give them a hug and tell them, "You are welcome here!" I learned that lesson from my friends in Uganda.

Throughout your life you will meet new people who visit your church or go to your school or join your sports teams. They will probably have been invited by someone to be there. Make them feel more than just invited—make them feel welcomed. There's a big difference between the two. If you've ever been new to something, maybe you moved to a new neighborhood or joined a team for the first time, you know how much it means for someone to include you. So return the favor and welcome others into your friend group!

One of our jobs in Jesus' kingdom is to be *hosts*—to make people feel welcome when they come. While we can definitely invite people, we don't get to make decisions about who is in and who is out. Instead, we get to stand at the door, give hugs, and remind everyone we greet, "You are welcome here!"

36
GRACE AND TOILET PAPER

When my kids were in middle school, toilet papering was really popular. Other students would pull this prank at night by sneaking into someone's yard and covering the trees and bushes with toilet paper. There are a few good reasons that you really shouldn't TP someone's house—it wastes paper and makes a big mess that someone else has to clean up. Even so, it happened to us a couple times, and our kids thought it was hilarious to walk out in the morning to a completely white front yard. I thought it was pretty funny too because I knew that the kids who were playing the prank didn't mean to do any harm. The TP war between the kids' middle school friends raged for a few months until it finally went too far.

One night, our house and yard were covered in toilet paper. We happened to be doing construction on a part of our house at the time, and several construction workers were at our house during the day, so we had a porta-potty set up in the driveway. While a group of my son's friends were covering the house with toilet paper, someone thought it would be funny to tip over the porta-potty. I know I don't have to explain the mess to you—it wasn't funny *at all*.

We had a good idea about where these kids were staying that night, so in the morning I called the house and told the dad what had happened. He loaded all the boys into his car and came to our house. I think they expected to be in big trouble or be yelled at. The boys assembled on our lawn with their heads hanging low, feeling pretty awful for what they had done. While I walked out to greet them, Sweet Maria slipped out to run an errand.

I definitely wasn't happy about what had happened in my yard, but I didn't give the boys the lecture they were expecting. Instead, I talked with them about how they were growing into men. I said that boys who are becoming men (and girls who are becoming women, for that matter) are defined by how they show respect for others. Everyone can have some fun, but they had disrespected my home and my family by taking a prank too far. I told them we were going to work together to make it right. The boys all apologized, and of course, I forgave them. My sons jumped in to help, and we all worked side by side to get that mess off the driveway.

Just as we were wrapping up, Sweet Maria pulled our car back into the driveway. What the boys didn't know was that she had gone on a mission to buy dozens of donuts—the really good kind covered in sprinkles. With a smile, she said, "We're calling this a repentance party. Who's ready for breakfast?"

Everyone got cleaned up, and we sat on the back porch

together having orange juice and donuts. What started out as a situation where everyone felt pretty awful quickly changed because we all wanted to make things right. My sons became even better friends with the boys who made a mess in the front of our house, and interestingly enough, those kids didn't play pranks like that anymore.

Jesus talked a lot about what we should do when people hurt us or let us down. Did you know that other people will know we are friends with Jesus when they see the way we treat those who are mean to us? Jesus said that if someone does something to hurt us, we shouldn't hurt them back. Instead, we should meet acts of meanness or insensitivity with acts of *kindness*. What I've learned from Jesus is when someone does something to hurt us, we need to give them a chance to make things right. By responding with kindness instead of hurting others back, we often become even better friends with them and get to show them the kindness of Jesus.

37

TIPPY TOES

When my sister and I were kids, our parents tracked how tall we were by standing us against a doorframe and drawing little lines over our heads. I always thought I was a little taller than my sister, but she was older than me and proudly pointed out that she was a little taller too. After my parents marked the doorframe, I would step back eagerly to see if I had caught up to my sister. I was a tall, lanky kid, so I knew I would outgrow her soon. It just never seemed to happen, though.

Finally, the day came when I just *knew* my little mark on the door would be taller than hers. I stood next to my sister, peering down at the top of her head, and I couldn't wait to see my mark high up on the doorframe. But when I stepped back from the door, I saw that my mark was just a little lower than hers. *How could that be?!* I was sure I had her by an inch *at least*. It just didn't make sense. I would have bet all my candy store money that I was taller.

I'm not completely sure why measuring myself against my sister mattered so much to me. We all do it. We measure ourselves against our friends or athletes or the popular kids at school or famous singers. We see how close we are to them. Are they just an inch better than us? Two inches? God never

meant it to be this way. He made each of us to be someone different. He doesn't want us to measure ourselves against anyone but Him and His extravagant love.

I begged my parents to measure my sister and me just one more time. My sister backed up against the doorframe, and my parents got the pencil out again. This time I noticed something: I saw that she was standing *on her tippy toes!* For years, she'd been pretending to be an inch taller than she really was.

As I've grown up, I've noticed that no matter how big or small we are, we all want to feel special and loved and important. Sometimes we try to look like the best in order to feel those good feelings. We may dress or act a certain way just because other people are doing it. When we do these things, we're really just trying to be an inch taller than someone else. Many people live their entire lives on their tippy toes, so to speak, and it can be a pretty exhausting way to live.

As I've gotten to know Jesus more, I've realized that those things I really wanted—things like love and specialness—are things I already have. You have them too. When Jesus sees you, He already loves you from your head to your toes. You don't need to stretch up higher on your tippy toes for Him to like you more. You don't need to measure yourself against anything or anyone. You don't have to be taller or smarter or funnier to be loved by God. You are already loved and accepted, just for being exactly who God made you to be.

38

QUITTER

When I was young, a lot of grown-ups gave me advice. They would say things like "Don't give up!" and "Don't quit!"

In most situations, this is great advice. It's advice I would give to my own kids at one point or another. When it came to studying for spelling tests, learning to drive, or being nice to someone who wasn't nice to them, my advice was always the same: "Don't quit! You can do it!"

I really took the idea of never quitting to heart, and I started to say yes to everything. I'm sure you know by now that I usually think more of anything is better. More balloons, more time, more trips to Disneyland, and definitely more sprinkles on donuts. For years, I said yes to everything! But you know what? I was *so* busy and my life was *so* full that I started to worry I was doing a lot of different things, but some of those things didn't really matter. I needed to make a big change in my life so I had room for the important stuff.

I decided to declare Thursdays as "Quit Something Day." I quit one thing every Thursday. I'm not kidding! I quit things like helping lead an organization or complaining or eating marshmallows. It could be anything! I even quit my job one Thursday. I started to realize that in order to have time for

the most important things in my life, I needed to be willing to let go of a lot of other things. What's funny is that even though some of the things I quit were bad for me in the first place, lots of them were things that might be good for someone else . . . but they were making me too busy to do the things Jesus was inviting me to.

Did you know that Jesus told His friends to be quitters too? He said to *run* from things that might cause us to grow apart from Him. He said to quit looking at things that weren't good for us to see and to quit taking things that aren't ours. He told His friends to quit doing things that were unkind. The Bible talks about a man named Paul who was one of the first leaders of the Church. Paul said that we should quit doing anything that causes someone else to be confused about who God is and how much He loves us. The Bible is full of advice about what things we should keep doing and what things we should quit. Now, there are some things in life you shouldn't ever quit, like loving or forgiving people. Definitely don't give up on those things. There are other things, though, that we should always feel free to quit. Here are a few examples you can practice right now:

Quit worrying.

Quit fighting with your brother or sister.

Quit being afraid.

If we quit the things that aren't God's best for us, maybe we will have more time for things that matter. I picked Thursday as my day to quit things, but you could pick any day you want! What are some things you could quit today so you'll have more time for the good things Jesus wants for you?

39

THREE MINUTES AT A TIME

I travel a lot for my job, and I spend a lot of time in airports. Most of the time when I go somewhere, I am on the first flight of the day, which means I'm at the airport at the same time each morning.

It wasn't long before I started recognizing the faces of people who worked at the airport. One man in particular caught my eye. He checked IDs, like driver's licenses and passports, to see if people really were who they said they were before they got on their airplanes. What stood out to me about this man was how he always seemed to be overflowing with joy, even at five o'clock in the morning. He was very small and wiry, and I liked to imagine that the wrinkles on his face came from years of smiling ear to ear.

One morning as he was checking my ID, I told him my name was Bob and asked what his was. He looked up at me as he gave me my driver's license back and said with his usual smile, "I'm Adrian!"

"Adrian," I said, "I've got to tell you—every morning I come to the airport, and you're the first person I see. You are so full of joy. You remind me a lot of Jesus." Adrian flashed

another huge smile, and without saying anything, he gave me a big bear hug. His head came up to about my belly button. The whole conversation couldn't have lasted more than three minutes or so, but I knew I had just made a new friend.

From then on, whenever I went through security, I could count on Adrian smiling at me, giving me a hug, and checking my ID to make sure I was really Bob. Over the following months, I found out—three minutes at a time—that Adrian and his wife had just moved to San Diego from Tijuana, Mexico. For decades before the move, he had been an airplane mechanic. I heard about his children and grandchildren and how his wife baked big batches of cookies and sold them so that they could have enough money for groceries.

Soon Adrian became friends with our whole family. We spent several Christmases together. When my daughter, Lindsey, grew up and moved away to college, she would see Adrian in the security line at the airport, and he would rush over, smiling, and yell, "Young lady! How are you? Travel safe back to school!"

Because we lived right by the airport, Adrian would come over to our house whenever he took a long break at work. Even though it was a friendship that began only three minutes at a time, Adrian continued to be part of our family for many years. I think God made it that way on purpose to remind us that we don't need years or weeks or even days to become friends with someone. The next time you're waiting in line to use the monkey bars at school or get your lunch in the cafeteria, look around you! You just might make a new friend. Most of the time, all it takes is three minutes.

(40)

THE PUPPETEER

When my daughter, Lindsey, was growing up, one of our favorite things to do together was to look at art galleries. She loved to paint, so on Saturday mornings we would get up early, stop at a coffee shop to grab some hot chocolate, and

walk around to different galleries to get ideas for her next creation. The art galleries were pretty fancy places, and we would both stare in awe at the beautiful, detailed paintings that some really talented people had made.

One day, Lindsey and I walked through a gallery together, and I stopped short when I saw the most magnificent painting I'd ever seen hanging on a wall. The name of the painting was *The Puppeteer*. It was a painting of a grandpa sitting at a dinner table with his family. The grandpa was putting on a puppet show with a huge smile on his face. Toys were scattered on the floor where the children had abandoned them, and dishes were left in the sink. It seemed that everyone had immediately dropped whatever they were doing to watch the grandpa put on a puppet show. I loved the painting because it reminded me of how much I love spending time with my own family. It also reminded me of how Jesus invites us to gather around His table too.

I decided that the painting had to be mine, so I started to save up. It took a long time before I had enough money set aside to buy the painting. Finally, the day came, and I raced to the gallery with my money in hand.

When I arrived, I was surprised to see *two* paintings that looked exactly the same sitting proudly on easels—they were both the same painting of the puppeteer! I asked the man at the gallery why I was getting two paintings.

"The painting on the left," he said, "is the real one. The one on the right is the copy."

It turns out that if you buy a really nice painting, you actually get two. The copy is the one you are supposed to put up on your wall for everyone to see, and the original painting is supposed to go in a secret vault so nothing bad happens to it. Have you ever heard of such a silly thing? Of course, you know the one I hung on my wall—the real one! I bet you would have too. I understand why the man at the gallery

wanted me to hang the fake painting up. The original was a priceless masterpiece. What if you put the real one on the wall, and it got damaged?

Now, here's something you need to know about our house: if you ever come visit, you'd better come armed. When I bought *The Puppeteer*, my kids all had rubber-band guns, and we had some epic battles.

One morning, as I was sitting down in the living room to drink my coffee, I looked up at *The Puppeteer* and almost spilled the entire cup on myself. The puppeteer had taken a hit from a rubber band—*right in the head!* The kids all promised up and down that they didn't do it, but I'm a dad. I know these things. My priceless painting was a casualty of a rubber-band war.

I could have been really mad that my priceless painting got a ding, but you know what? I wasn't. The little mark on the puppeteer's forehead makes me like the painting even more.

Just like hanging a priceless painting on the wall, showing the real version of ourselves is a little scary sometimes. We're afraid we won't be accepted or that we'll be hurt or damaged by someone else. So instead, we put a fake version of ourselves up on display rather than the real one. We know it's not real, but we pretend to be real in front of other people while we hide our real selves—the masterpiece—somewhere safe. Do you know what God thinks we should do with our masterpiece?

He doesn't want us to hide it anymore. He doesn't want us to play it safe. In fact, no amount of rubber-band marks could change the fact that you are God's masterpiece, and those little imperfections you get along the way make Him love you even more. Don't be afraid to show the real you, because you are God's masterpiece!

41

FOR EACH OTHER

When my kids were growing up, we had a rule in our family: any time the kids stood up for one of their siblings, the whole family would have a party. Thankfully, we got to have a lot of parties because our kids learned early on that we stand up for each other. Even though getting along with brothers or sisters or friends can be hard, I knew that if they stuck up for each other, they would be good friends for the rest of their lives.

When my daughter, Lindsey, was in high school, one of her friends passed away. It was a shock to everyone. Death is a really sad and hard thing to cope with. It makes God sad too. When you're grieving the loss of someone, you might feel a wave of emotions hit you out of nowhere, and you'll start to feel really sad. That's normal, but even knowing that doesn't make it any easier to go through.

As the family sat around the dinner table one night, we talked about how sad it was that Lindsey lost her friend. We were all feeling heavy-hearted for Lindsey and for her friend's family. As we talked, I turned to my boys and said, "Sons, Lindsey is going to be feeling really sad for a while, and it might hit her at different times. Your job is to protect your sister's heart. If she begins missing her friend a lot and starts

to cry, comfort her. If she looks sad and you think she needs a distraction, make one. If she needs someone to just sit next to her and be quiet, have a seat. As her family, we all get to take care of her."

Do you know what my sons did? Of course you do, because you would do the exact same thing. My sons looked out for their sister during a hard time. Sometimes all we can do is to walk *through* sadness with each other, not around it. God gave us each other so we wouldn't need to pass through the most difficult times alone.

Nowadays, my kids are all grown up, and they live in the same city. And you know what? They're best friends. The commitment they made as kids to be there for each other continues to this day. They stood up for each other then, and they still look out for each other now. One of them will get sick or need help moving or have a hard day at work, and they're all there for each other. It's years later, but Sweet Maria and I still get to have lots of parties. You know why? Because our kids stick up for each other.

Did you know that right before Jesus died, He prayed for His friends? That includes all of the people who would follow Him one day, including us! Jesus didn't pray that we would get everything we always wanted or that things would be easy for us. Instead, He prayed that God would help us love each other well. He prayed that we would act like we were all *one* person. Jesus meant that He wanted us to stick together. If one person was hurt, we would all feel hurt. If one person was happy, we would all celebrate. Jesus prayed that our joy in Him would be complete and said that we would only know what complete joy felt like when we loved one another the way He loved us. Have you ever thought about how the way you treat your fam-ily members could be one of the greatest ways you can show the world about God's love?

SECRETLY INCREDIBLE

Have you ever seen the movie *The Incredibles*? It's about a family with superpowers that has to learn how to use those powers together.

The father, Mr. Incredible, meets with a woman named Edna, whose job is to make superhero outfits. When discussing the design of his new suit, Edna keeps repeating this advice: "No capes." Mr. Incredible is clearly disappointed because he really wants a uniform with a cape (wouldn't you?), but Edna stands her ground. She even gives examples of the problems capes can cause—they get caught in elevator shafts and vortexes. Her point is simple: capes can get in the way of heroes doing awesome stuff. I think Jesus agrees.

When Jesus was here on Earth teaching and healing people, do you know what He said after He performed a big miracle for someone? He told the person, "Don't tell anyone." Instead of making a big deal out the amazing things He was doing, Jesus wanted to keep them quiet—and when He did that, He showed us how we should act too. It was almost like Jesus chose not to wear a cape.

One time, Jesus met two people who were blind—they

couldn't see a thing! Do you know what Jesus told them after He healed them? "Don't say anything to anyone." Now, if *I* had just healed someone who couldn't see, I would tell everyone! I'd make shirts and bumper stickers and probably ask for my own TV show. Come to think of it, I want to ask for my own TV show when I remember to mow the lawn!

Jesus was talking with His friends and told them, "You know, if you really want to be like Me, here's what you need to do. If you do something good, don't make a big deal out of it. Don't do nice things for people so that you'll get attention. Instead, do great things for other people *in secret* because God always sees what you do!"

This is how we should act.

When we try to get a lot of attention for the good things we do, it's like we're putting on a cape. But here's the thing: capes can make us trip and fall and forget the most important reasons why we are here. The reason you and I are here on Earth is to love God and love the people around us. When we lose our capes, we stop trying to look like action figures and we become something far more important to God; we become *secretly incredible.* Secretly incredible people keep what they do one of God's best-kept secrets because He's the only One who needs to know.

God has created all of us to do great things. We are all heroes and servants in His eyes. When Jesus helped others quietly, He was showing the people around Him that our lives are not all about us. We don't need to wear a cape or tell everyone about the good things we're doing. When we don't make it about us, we can point people's attention to Jesus.

43

A NEW HEART

People who love Jesus talk about how God gives us a new heart, but I never really understood what that meant until I met my friend Kelly.

Kelly is one of the most adventurous people I know. She's not much bigger than you are, but she's built out of courage and fearlessness from head to toe. She isn't scared of heights at all—in fact, she *loves* climbing as high as she can. Kelly's favorite thing to do with her husband is to climb mountains. As if that weren't amazing enough, Kelly has a *brand-new heart.* Let me tell you how this happened.

You see, some years ago, Kelly's heart got really sick. It wasn't working the way it was supposed to. Kelly's doctors said her heart wasn't going to last much longer and that she would need to get a new one. The amazing thing about these doctors is that they knew exactly what to do to help Kelly. She had to have a big surgery, and I bet that made her feel pretty nervous. But you know what? It worked! Kelly's brand-new heart started beating in her chest, and she was stronger than ever.

Kelly's new heart works a little differently from yours or mine, though. Put your hand on your chest right now. Do you feel your heart beating in there? Now do ten jumping jacks and feel your heart again. Is it beating a little faster? I

bet it is. God uses nerves connected to our hearts to tell our brains how fast our hearts should beat. When we run and jump and move really fast, our brains send messages to our hearts telling them to beat faster to keep up with us. When our hearts pump blood faster, they send oxygen to our whole body, which is what we need when we're playing hard. When we sit still again, our hearts slow back down. Our brains and hearts work together to keep us healthy and strong this way. What made Kelly's new heart different from yours and mine is that her brain didn't know how to talk to her new heart.

When Kelly would try to climb a mountain, her new heart would have trouble speeding up to get all the oxygen she needed. Do you think that stopped Kelly from climbing mountains? Of course not! Instead, she learned to whisper to her heart.

When Kelly starts to climb a mountain and needs her heart to beat faster, she tells her heart, "This is going to be really hard work. We're climbing, and you need to beat really fast!" and her heart obeys. Kelly has another problem when she gets to the top of a mountain. Her heart still thinks she's climbing! So Kelly whispers to her heart again, "We made it! You can rest now."

The Bible says that God makes us into new creations. Here's another way to put it: God has placed brand-new hearts inside of us. Have you ever stopped to think that the words that you say to yourself and your heart are really important? Just like Kelly talks to her heart, we get to talk to our own new hearts and remind ourselves about who God is and who He made us to be.

Take a moment to remind your heart that God loves you, that He'll take care of you, and that He knows you by name. If you're tired, tell your heart that it can rest in Jesus. If you're feeling afraid, remind your heart that God is always with you and He will never leave you. If you've been working really hard, whisper to your heart about that too. God wants to know how you and your new heart are doing.

CROC DROP

"Bob, our church is having a croc drop. Do you want to come?"

"A croc drop!?" I said, surprised and delighted. "I'm in!"

I had no idea what a croc drop was, but it sounded awesome. I hung up the phone with the pastor from Alabama who had just invited me to speak at his church and see this croc drop, whatever that was. I have never seen a real crocodile before, except one time in a movie, and I pictured how cool it would be to see hundreds of crocodiles dropping from the ceiling. I figured that's what happens at a croc drop.

When I got to Alabama and met up with the pastor, I could feel my excitement building as we walked toward a big warehouse where the meeting was going to happen. I hoped the crocs hadn't been dropped already, and if they had, that maybe a few were still hiding up in the rafters.

When I walked into the warehouse, I was a little confused. There were rows and rows of tables with piles of potatoes, and there were lots of people—but no crocodiles.

After a couple of awkward moments looking around, I got up the courage to ask my new pastor friend, "So, where are the crocodiles, and where do they drop from?"

My friend looked at me for a second, half-grinning, and cocked his head. "Crocodiles?"

"Yeah," I said. "You know . . . for the croc drop."

A huge grin grew over his face, and he exploded into a belly laugh. "Bob, this isn't a croc drop. It's a *crop* drop!"

The warehouse wasn't full of crocodiles, after all. It was full of *crops*. Crops are what we call the food that farmers grow in their fields. All the different churches in the area walked through the fields to gather together any of the crops the farmers' machines missed. They worked together to pack the food into bags and gave them to people in the community who were hungry.

Here's the beautiful thing about what was happening in that room: if you had asked someone what church they were from, they wouldn't have told you the name of the church they went to on Sunday morning. They would have just said, "Our church!" Sometimes it's easy to forget that Jesus' church isn't a bunch of separate churches that meet in different buildings. It's one church that meets in lots of places. We're all like a big family in this way. The amazing thing about Jesus is that He came to draw people close to Him and close to each other so that we can help one another. Jesus will use whatever it takes to bring us together too—whether it's a bunch of potatoes or a roof full of crocodiles.

45

BRAVE

I have a friend named Charlie, and he is very brave.

Charlie is a little boy from Uganda who lived with his mother in a home far from any big cities. When Charlie was ten years old, something bad happened to him. Some people hurt his body. But here's the thing about Charlie—he is a strong little boy. Even though some people hurt him, Charlie was brave enough to get help. He told his mom and the police and other safe grown-ups in his life what had happened to him, and that's how we met.

Because I'm a lawyer, I get to help kids by making sure people follow laws. When I met Charlie and heard his story, I thought I could help him. We found the people who hurt Charlie and put them in jail.

That might seem like the end of the story, but we had big plans for helping Charlie. Charlie needed to see a doctor, and some doctors in California volunteered to help him. So it was settled—Charlie was headed to America for the very first time! Before we left Uganda, Charlie and I went to the courthouse in Uganda together to get permission for him to travel with me.

Charlie and I went to the airport in Uganda and got on a huge airplane. Because Charlie had grown up in a village in

Uganda, far from the city, he'd never even seen an airplane before. Charlie was surprised and excited when the airplane flew into the sky with both of us on board!

Uganda is a long way from the United States, so we stopped in London, England, to take a break. This country has kings and queens and guards who wear big hats. When we got off the plane, I checked my phone, and guess who

had sent me a message. The White House! I'm not kidding. The people at the White House had heard all about Charlie and how brave he was, and their message was short. Here's what it said: "We'd like to meet Charlie!" So, do you know what we did? We flew to Washington, DC, and went to the president's house. Imagine what it would be like to be out in the jungle in Uganda one day and standing in the Oval Office the next!

After we left the White House, we flew across the country to meet the doctors for Charlie's operation. It went great, and Charlie got better. Having surgery isn't that fun, so right after Charlie got out of the hospital, I told him about a tradition we have in our family. When each of my kids turns ten, they get to pick an adventure to go on with me. They get to go wherever they want to go. When Lindsey turned ten, she wanted to have a tea party in London. Richard wanted to climb Half Dome, which is a huge rock in Yosemite, and Adam wanted to ride motorcycles in the desert. Do you know what Charlie said he wanted to do for his ten-year-old adventure? He wanted to climb Mount Kilimanjaro!

In case you don't know, Mount Kilimanjaro is the tallest mountain in Africa and one of the tallest mountains in the whole world. A lot of airplanes don't even fly as high as this mountain.

"Are you really sure you want to climb Mount Kilimanjaro,

Charlie? What if we just go to Disneyland instead?" I asked with a laugh.

"No. Let's climb Mount Kilimanjaro!" Charlie said again. So we did!

Neither of us knew how to climb a big mountain like Mt. Kilimanjaro, but we had some friends who did, so we went with them. When we got to the base camp at the bottom of the mountain, we were still taking the price tags off our new boots and jackets. I started to wonder if we had made a big mistake. Up until then, I had been worried about whether Charlie would be able to climb this big mountain. Looking up at it, though, I began to wonder if *I* could climb it.

We grabbed our gear and started up the trail. Charlie was a trooper. We hiked together during the days and we shivered together in our freezing cold tent during the nights. Charlie almost made it all the way to the top. I was so proud of him. When we got as high up the mountain as Charlie could go, we had a ceremony.

I like to carry around medals with me everywhere I go, because if the world needs one thing, it's more heroes. I pinned the first medal to Charlie's little jacket and said, "Charlie, you are *brave*."

I pulled out another medal, pinned it to him, and said, "Charlie, you are *courageous*."

I pulled out another and did the same, saying, "Charlie, you are *fearless*."

I had fifteen medals with me, so I put all of them on Charlie's jacket. When Charlie walked down that mountain, his jacket was weighed down with brightly colored, clanking medals. He jingled when he walked.

Charlie had made it to *his* summit. Instead of telling him how much farther he needed to go, we stopped to celebrate how far he had come. I think God does that for us every day. He sees the hard things in our lives. He walks beside us and asks us to look at how far we've come with Him. We get to do that for each other too.

What are some ways that you could celebrate how far you have come, and how far you have seen others come?

46

WAVING TO JESUS

When I started spending time in Uganda, my Ugandan friends and I would visit villages out in the bush. That means that we were really far away from big cities. One time after spending the afternoon in the bush, we got into our Jeep and started to drive back to the house where we were staying. A few of the local kids ran after the Jeep as we drove away, and I waved to them and said good-bye. Then more kids started running after the car, so I started waving even faster. By the time dozens of kids were running after the car, I was waving with both hands, trying to make sure that each kid got a wave. This only made even more kids follow us!

I turned to the driver of the Jeep and said, "Wow, these kids are so friendly! I wonder why they're chasing us?"

My Ugandan friend glanced over to my side of the car, watching me wave at the kids, and he burst into laughter. "Bob!" he said with a huge smile and a laugh. "In America, a wave like that means good-bye, but here it means you're asking them to follow you!"

When Jesus was here on Earth, He went from town to town and invited the people He met to follow Him. It was like He was waving to them Ugandan-style, saying, "Follow me!" Some of the people Jesus met understood what He meant,

and they followed after Him. Still others just waved back at Him. It wasn't that they didn't like Jesus. They simply didn't understand that He wasn't just saying hello or good-bye. He was inviting them to follow Him.

Jesus is doing the same for you and me every day. He's inviting us to follow Him. And we get to decide whether we're just going to wave back or if we're going to follow Him. What will you choose?

ABOUT THE AUTHORS

BOB GOFF is the founder of Love Does, a non-profit organization that operates schools and pursues justice for children in conflict areas such as Uganda, Somalia, and Iraq. Bob is a lawyer and serves as the honorary consul for the Republic of Uganda to the United States. He is an adjunct professor at Pepperdine Law School and Point Loma Nazarene University and lives in San Diego with Sweet Maria, their kids, and their extended family.

LINDSEY GOFF VIDUCICH loves kids. She began her teaching career at a therapeutic childcare center in Seattle and went on to teach kindergarten in Nashville, first grade in Salem, Oregon, and both first and second grades in San Diego. Lindsey lives with her husband, Jon, and spends most of her free time creating art and living new stories with her family.